Griefbox and other plays

SUSAN BRADLEY SMITH was born in Bega, NSW, Australia and educated at the universities of New South Wales and New England, and the National Institute of Dramatic Arts (Playwright's Studio). She is the co-author of *Playing With Ideas: Australian Women Playwrights from the Suffragettes to the Sixties* and editor of *Tremendous Worlds: Australian Women's Drama 1890–1960*, and lives in London where she teaches Australian Studies at Kings College, University of London.

Griefbox
and other plays

SUSAN BRADLEY SMITH

PUBLISHED BY SALT PUBLISHING
PO Box 202, Applecross, Western Australia 6153
PO Box 937, Great Wilbraham, Cambridge PDO CB1 5JX United Kingdom

First published 2001

Printed and bound in the United Kingdom by Lightning Source

Typeset in Swift 9.5 / 13

British Library Cataloguing-in-Publication Data
A catalogue record for this book is available from the British Library
ISBN 1 876857 17 X paperback

SP

1 3 5 7 9 8 6 4 2

to Matthias

Contents

Acknowledgements

I once read in the acknowledgements to one of the first feminist histories of Australia a backhanded thanks from the author to her colleagues for their insistent scepticism that such a history existed let alone was worth writing. In that spirit I would like to thank Sydney's National Institute of Dramatic Arts and their Playwright's Studio for all their criticism, tuition, fights and friendships, and of course the opportunity to have your plays performed, but especially my tutor Nicolas Parsons and my fellow student playwrights. Without that journey I would be a poorer writer than I am today. Waitressing has never been good for my writing, so I sincerely thank those people and institutions that made it possible for me to continue to write whilst pursuing other professional endeavours, including the Department of English at the University of New England (Julian Croft, for saying that I was a better playwright than scholar), the School of Writing at Southern Cross University, and the Menzies Centre for Australian Studies, King's College London, (where I've had to opportunity to meet and be moved by the work of more Australian writers than I deserve). Most of all I would like to thank those people close to me in my life who always inspire: my brother Graeme Smith (also for the cover photo that somehow perfectly matched a story he had never read); my former husband Matthias (not the least for having to suffer audiences believing he is the real-life villain of every play); Charlie Le Duff and Amy Kuzniar for the love and the lake; Julie Hancock for her unceasing, theatrical friendship; John Kinsella for his faith and conversation; and finally James Bradley, who knows it best.

Worry: a foreword

I hope this is the shortest foreword in history because to explain your writing seems like an unwelcome conceit, on all sides. But someone unexpected came into my life recently and at the witching hour I was asked where it came from, the writing. Because in answering I found out something I hadn't known I'll take that encounter as sign that an honest explanation is better than the more flattering concealments I had planned. In saying that I write from a place of pain, I write more because it takes me away from that place. Despite the grievous outcomes of many of my plays, it is the exploration of hope contained in the action that I want to have the most resonance. The promise of damage being repaired at personal and political levels is the seductive force that makes me bother. It seems that I bother most about the failure of love, the failure of communication, but it is also the world we try to love and communicate in that occupies me. The world I once knew best is Australia, so the emotional, psychological, physical and linguistic landscapes of my plays are more often than not Australian. And I write plays more than anything else for the perverse reason that they are the hardest thing for me to write, and because the struggle somehow corresponds to my subject matter, which emerges better from the fight. That, and watching an audience watch your play, which is a terrifying delight. Theatre frightens me, the collaboration, the actors, the audience, the so very public nature of the confessional, the way that it can sometimes effect real change. But it's one of the best things I know.

Griefbox

(seven locked monologues of grief, with witnesses)

Characters

These monologues could be performed by one actor, but they are designed for seven different actors with one griever and six witnesses (guardian angels) to each episode of grief.

WITNESSES / GUARDIAN ANGELS
PRINCESS, *a working mother*
THE BUS CONDUCTOR
ROBERT, *a smart young businessman*
THE BOSS
DENISE, *a recently widowed mother*
THE DAUGHTER
ELOISE, *a university student*
THE UNIVERSITY LECTURER
CAMERON, *a lonely man at a high school reunion*
THE FRIEND AT THE URINAL
MIRANDA, *an adulterer*
THE BARMAN
ROBERT, *an octogenarian*
THE BIRTHDAY GUESTS

Prologue

Dressed for a funeral, the actors enter one by one and join the original monologue, until it builds to choral proportions.

ALL

'In all truth I tell you, whoever listens to my words, and believes in the one sent me, has eternal life; without being brought to judgement such a person has passed from death to life. In all truth I tell you, the hour is coming – indeed it is already here – when the dead will hear the voice of the Son of God, and all who hear it will live. For as the Father has life in himself, so has he granted the Son also to have life in himself; and, because he is the Son of a man, has granted him power to give judgement. Do not be surprised at this, for the hour is coming when the dead will leave their graves at the sound of his voice: those who did good will come forth to life; and those who did evil will come forth to judgement'.

They all shake hands then exit.

Scene 1

The PRINCESS *hails and then sits on a bus. Enter* WITNESS.

WITNESS

Episode one: The Princess Who Lies.

WITNESS *joins the passengers.*

PRINCESS

Can you see that man? Down there. On the bicycle. His baby seat is empty. Who'd ride through this bloody traffic with a baby? Bloody idiot. Stupid bloody pom. Anyway. It's empty. The kid is safe somewhere I suppose. Already started its perfect day at its perfect nursery in this perfect city in this perfect country and it's only 8.43 jesus fucking christ why isn't this bloody bus moving? I always sit on the top deck. People are very uncomposed from this view. Like, every single one of those women standing down there waiting . . .

WITNESS *plays the role of the* BUS CONDUCTOR.

BUS CONDUCTOR

Full up, no more sorry. Full up. There's another one coming right behind.

PRINCESS

Liar! . . . waiting to be allowed on, they, all of them, need to get themselves quick damn smart to the hairdresser and get their roots dyed. And Fred there, he needs to buy himself a decent dandruff shampoo. How people can just let themselves go like that I don't know. Shabby old town. I'm lucky to be here though. In the heart of the old empire and all. Lucky, really. Lucky to be on the bloody bus, let's face it. Some days I just can't stand it. The other day for example . . .

BUS CONDUCTOR

Fares please. Anymore fares please. Fares please.

PRINCESS

I got thrown off the bus. At the Angel.

BUS CONDUCTOR

I don't take no twenty pound notes lady.

PRINCESS

But it's all I have.

BUS CONDUCTOR

I don't have to take it.

PRINCESS

I can't ask the automatic teller for small change!

BUS CONDUCTOR

Get off at the next stop Lady and don't you get on no bus of mine again without the right money. Now get off or I'll stop the bus.

PRINCESS

Well. At first I refused to move. I ignored him. Was he picking on me because I was white? Then he got mad. Then I got mad. Said it was legal tender, and asked him to point out the signs warning people to have the right money or bloody else there were none of course and by this time he'd stopped the bus and was asking everyone to get off and people were abusing me, and others were offering to pay my fare for me and were criticising the conductor for his rudeness and excessive officiousness. I became hysterical. I became extremely dangerous. I screamed he was going to burn in hell for his cruelty, for my humiliation, his wrong-headedness, his inhumanity. He looked a bit worried. He refused to give me his name or number. I looked at all the other people and saw how frightened they were of my lunacy and how very close so many of them were to falling off my edge that I just turned and fled into the back streets of Islington.

BUS CONDUCTOR

Hold tight.

PRINCESS

I was very late for work.

WITNESS *becomes* PASSENGER.

PRINCESS

My bus. 'RML2460 JJD4CD. RML2460 was delivered to the new London transport area in May 1966. Its first garage was Northfleeting. After many years in the NL country area it was, in 1970, transferred to the new London Country Bus services. In 1979 it was withdrawn for scrap but London transport bought it back along with most other country RMLs (although 24 were sold to Wombwell Diesel's in Yorkshire and these were broken up before LT could buy them back. However the rest were bought, sent to Aldenham Works, were made serviceable and painted red and placed in service around London. RML2460 was allocated to Tottenham for use on Route 73. In 1990 its original AEL Engine was refurbished at Tottenham garage (mechanical work) and at Enfield Heavy repair Centre (body work). During the body refurb all the exterior panels were replaced and an inscription was found above the rear entrance saying 'RML2460, the last green one' and was signed by all the staff who built her. (Unfortunately this can not be seen but has been preserved by sealing with varnish.) This practice was a trademark of the Park-Royal Vehicles, that is, the first and last of every body type they built. RML2460 will continue to serve London for many years yet, and passengers on Route 73 daily. When she is finally withdrawn it is hoped that she will pass into preservation. Chassis AEC RRH A & B SUB Frames Engine Cummin's C series 8.2 135 BHP at 1800 RPM Transmission speed electro-pneumatic automatic gear box and Spiral Bevel Differential Body Park-Royal 72 seat doubledecker built in April 1966, Harlesdon, London, NW11.'

Silence

I do not have a daughter. Every morning, I do not leave her at this shitty nursery in a filthy north London suburb. Every single morning, she does not cry her heart out at the grubby window, watching me disappear behind piles of spewn rubbish to the bus shelter and I use that word loosely around the corner, where I never ever have to wait for the number 73 bus, and I always get a seat. I have a job in the city that makes all this worthwhile. I do not have debts, and I suffer no guilt.

Silence

When I finally withdraw from all this nothing, will I too pass into a state of preservation? Painted. Pickled with grief. And how do I pay for these sins I have not committed?

Bell rings. Bus stops. PRINCESS *leaves. Blackout.*

Scene 2

ROBERT, *a smart young businessman, stands before his boss who sits behind his big desk in an expensive office.*

WITNESS

Episode two: Robert Loses His Job.

WITNESS *plays the role of* ROBERT*'s boss, and makes paper aeroplanes during his monologue.*

ROBERT

You can't sack me because I'm late! This is not school mate. I mean, where do you get off behaving like this? I was here till nine o'clock last night closing that deal, and you sack me because I'm twenty minutes late! And so what, by the way, if I am a bit late, and so what, moreover, if I make a habit of it. You can't control the world for God's sake you should have seen the traffic this morning and to top it all off the bus stopped for ages because of this lunatic woman who didn't have any money and lost her rag at the conductor and you try getting a taxi at the Angel at that time of the morning so I just waited it out and for pity's sake I was working on the bus! Haven't you heard of the mobile phone! Eh? Eh? [*Silence*]

A paper aeroplane hits ROBERT.

You complete bastard. Have you any idea at all, the remotest inkling, what this is going to do to my family? There's a recession on out there, how's a man my age meant to find another job in an industry like this in a middle of a ruddy recession. [*Silence*] What is it? Tell me why you're really sacking me mate. Coward. Be a man. Be straight with me. What's wrong with me? What is wrong with me?

Another aeroplane hits ROBERT. *He picks it up off the floor, and crushes it in his hands. He leaves. Blackout.*

Scene 3

A wake. DENISE *is holding her young daughter.*

WITNESS

Episode three: Denise Tells Her Daughter Another Lie.

WITNESS *becomes* DENISE*'s daughter and sits in her lap.*

DENISE

Daddy's gone to heaven. Don't cry my baby. Daddy's gone to heaven. Daddy's gone to heaven. Daddy's gone to heaven. Daddy's gone to heaven. Daddy's gone to heaven. Don't cry my baby. Daddy's gone to heaven. Daddy's gone to heaven. Daddy's gone to heaven. Don't cry my baby. Don't cry my baby. Daddy's gone to heaven. Daddy's gone to heaven. Daddy's gone to heaven. Daddy's gone to heaven. Daddy's gone to heaven. Daddy's gone to heaven. Daddy's gone to heaven. Don't cry my baby. Daddy's gone to heaven. Daddy's gone to heaven. Daddy's gone to heaven. Daddy's gone to heaven. Oh please don't cry my baby.

Pause

DAUGHTER

Does Daddy still love us?

Silence

DENISE

'Breathe through the heats of our desire/Thy coolness and thy balm/Let sense be dumb, let flesh retire;/Speak through the earth-quake, wind and fire/O still small voice of calm!/O still small voice of calm.' Don't cry baby. Mummy loves you. Oh Lord hear our prayer.

DAUGHTER *leaves her mother's embrace. Blackout.*

Scene 4

A university lecture hall. ELOISE, *a student, begins taking notes but later stops.*

WITNESS

Episode four: Eloise abandons her university studies and takes up heroin.

WITNESS *is the* LECTURER.

LECTURER: ... Australian history contains not only a long history of racism but also a similar one of white activism protesting the crimes of colonisation. Patently, these protestations have not been effective enough. In 1991, Federal Parliament established the Council for Aboriginal Reconciliation to promote a formal process of reconciliation between indigenous Australians and the wider community, noting that the British Crown removed many indigenous peoples from their lands and that so far there has been no process for reconciliation. In 'governmentese', reconciliation is defined as 'working together to improve the relations between Aboriginal and Torres Strait Islander peoples and the rest of Australians'. The council is currently working on a draft document of reconciliation that has been hotly contested in public meetings throughout Australia, with the hope that such a document will contribute to 'a better Australia and better community relations so that all Australians can benefit.' This 'benefit for all' factor is the one that much of middle Australia remains to be convinced about, despite the fact that the situation for indigenous Australians, in general, is 'far less advantageous with respect to health, education, housing and income' than it is for non-indigenous Australians. Some of the things the Council think should be included in the document are as follows, and they define in principle the aspirations of reconciliation: Recognition about the unique status of the first Australians; The importance of land and culture to indigenous Australians; Respect for the continuing customary laws, beliefs and traditions of indigenous peoples; Acknowledgement that consent was neither sought nor given at the time of colonisation; Acknowledgement of indigenous history and its continuing consequences today; Greater equity in economic and social conditions for indigenous peoples; Strategies to ensure that reconciliation is included in government strategies so it becomes a reality. This all sounds very nice doesn't it. Positive. But here's a reality check. As one journalist recently reported from the Gallery, the repeated claim in Question Time was that 'Race issues are being cynically used to divide the Australian community for political purposes'. John Howard, in answer to the Opposition's questions about the Government's position on Aboriginal issues, accused Labor of 'maintaining differences of opinion over indigenous affairs as a divisive political issue in the Australian community'. In another newspaper article titled 'Politics of hate shames all Australians', the journalist said that 'I've started to wish that Sydney had never won the right to host the Olympics, so intent does the Howard Government seem on using the moment it affords us in the international spotlight to flush our global reputation down the toilet'. Solutions require leadership, and the Howard Government is providing little of that it seems. Recent history, and the rise of right wing sentiments in Australia, should make it obvious that reconciliation and its agenda strikes many a dissonant chord with too many Australians. This is precisely why those in positions of influence with a commitment to justice should be fully participating in reconciliation politics, even if only for the selfish, white-centred notion . . .

ELOISE *walks to the exit, banging the large door, shocking the lecturer into momentary silence.*

WITNESS

The, um, the yes the white centred notion of being able to consider your country's reputation with pride. After all, as Ruby Langford Ginibi said about the future for black and white Australians, 'There's got to be a coming together of the two because we're not going to go away, we've been here for ever and ever'. So, to my first question . . .

Blackout

Scene 5

Men's toilets in a Retired Serviceman's League club, host to a high school reunion. Refrain of old school song being drunkenly sung can be heard.

WITNESS

Episode five: Cameron Gets Bored at His High School Reunion.

WITNESS *joins* CAMERON *at the urinals.*

CAMERON: There's my mate Andy, who's a woodwork teacher, but he lives in Rooty Hill for christsakes, wouldn't come to Bondi for a beer on a Friday afternoon if his life depended on it. Which it does, probably, 'cause his wife is a champion weight-lifter or something and has a serious schedule up on the fridge and woe betide husband or child to fuck up that organisational masterpiece. Then there's Chris who runs the café down at Bronte beach and has a serious problem acting his age, always out with his young foreign waitresses (Aussie girls tend to recognise a dickhead when they see one) which is only fun about once every month so he's not much use as a mate these days. And bloody Robert, jesus, he disappeared for a few months, turns out he'd been up in Blackheath on some bloody meditation retreat from which he emerged solid in the knowledge that he had to join the local men's group and run around the Blue Mountains in the nuddy with spears getting back in touch with his inner man. And there's Sam, but poofters tend to prefer hanging out with other poofters, and I shouldn't forget Mark I suppose. He's alright. He never phones me these days but. And then there's me. [*Pause*] I miss the country. Sydney's a bit of an unfriendly place after a while.

Pause. They finish pissing, shake off, zip up.

CAMERON

Yeah. Anyway. So how's things with you Thommo?

Blackout

Scene 6

MIRANDA *is alone in a bar. The* WITNESS *is the* BARMAN.

WITNESS

Episode six: Miranda is unfaithful.

Barman pours her another drink.

MIRANDA

Cliche number one, 'love at first sight'. Cameron was head of the art department at the high school where I was sent to do my first practical as a trainee Commerce and Geography teacher. By the end of those three weeks he'd seduced me. He was so different from everyone else, his fingernails were dirty with a different coloured paint clogged up under each nail, and he smelt like daffodils. I agreed to let him paint me, that's how it started, he pestered me so much, and besides, I thought I'd never see him again. I knew that I'd never be a teacher. The last Friday night before I left, it happened. Everything. In the art storeroom, knocking over all the efforts of the year ten pottery class waiting for the kiln. I was deeply in love by the end of it, with shards of clay in my back. Cliche number two, 'The Guilt-free Abortion'. He never wrote, not once in months. I kept on with my studies until the morning I threw up all over an essay I had just finished typing. Three weeks later I had an abortion, in Balmain. Some feminist place. I went home to Surry Hills and drank beer with this pimply boy who'd just moved in to our joint and couldn't believe his luck. Then I got depressed. I adjusted my bra straps to a kind of grieving comfort. A month or so later Cameron came around with some flowers. Talking about unfinished business. He didn't talk too much though and he waited until he'd finished my painting before he ever kissed me properly. He made me look like someone else. Radiant and mysterious. Beautiful. Anyway. I finished my exams, he romanced me, my heart thawed out a bit, I got sick of playing scrabble with people who thought that three years teaching in the bush would build their character and even sicker of sleeping with them so we got married and I went to live with Cameron in his joint not far from where I'd had the old bubaloo scraped out. I've never set foot inside a high school again, and never once forgotten to take my pill. Cliche number three, 'I'm a very lucky person, I have no right to complain'. Once I lived near the beach. I swam beyond the breakers. Once I'm sure I had parents who must have fleetingly loved me. Once I went for a long ride on a motorbike without a helmet. Once I could remember the love of a man who twirled me round and round a rainbow, and asked me to stay. And once, one time, I felt the pressure of a growing foetus on my bladder. [*Silence*] I can feel my heart shrinking, so I know it's working.

MIRANDA *skulls her drink.*

MIRANDA
So. This very, very lucky girl's got a party to get to.

She exits. Blackout.

Scene 7

ROBERT'*s 80th birthday party.*

WITNESS
Episode seven: Robert's reprise.

ROBERT *quietens the cheers.*

WITNESS
Speech, speech!

ROBERT
Well, seeing as I'm 80 today and this might be my last chance, I might as well oblige you with a speech. Unaccustomed as I am. I remember when I was a young man and called upon to make a speech here and there, having the gift of the gab as I did, it was always the same speech to be suffered, not being the most original of blokes god put on the bloody earth. It must have been a good one though 'cause they kept asking me to talk. Anyhow. It goes like this. If I hold out both hands,

towards life, towards the heavens, and I dream in one hand and I shit in the other, which one will fill up first? Yeah yeah. Thank you. People always did laugh at that. The stinking truth that our lives are full of shit. We all know don't we. But it's worth it, eh. Seeing your little ones grow up and live a happier life than we have. Not worth topping yourself over, is it, a shitful existence. I'm still here. Aren't I? Anyway. Thanks for coming. It's nice to know you care. Cheers.

ROBERT *blows out his birthday cake candles to a gentle clapping. Blackout.*

Coda

At their resting place. The angel witnesses make ready to sleep so by the end of the scene they are all prostrate. All but one have removed their wings.

ALL

'Do not model yourselves on the behaviour of the world around you, but let your behaviour change, modelled by your new mind. This is the only way to discover the will of God and know what is good, what it is that God wants, what is the perfect thing to do. In the light of the grace I have received, I want to urge each one among you not to exaggerate your real importance. Each of you must judge yourself soberly by the standard of faith God has given you. Just as each of our bodies has several parts and each part has a separate function, so all of us, in union with Christ, form one body, as parts of it we belong to each other. Our gifts differ according to the grace given us. If your gift is prophecy, then use it as your faith suggests; if administration, then use it for administration; if teaching, then use it for teaching. Let the preachers deliver sermons, the almsgivers give freely, the officials be diligent, and those who do works of mercy do them cheerfully. Do not let your love be a pretence, but sincerely prefer good to evil. Love each other as much as brothers and sisters should, and have a profound respect for each other. . . Do not give up if trials come; and keep on praying'.

Silence

ANGEL

[*Taking off wings*] Who was that prayer for?

No answer. They sleep. Blackout.

THE END

The Bitch Trilogy

Filth and glamour

This is the first play in 'The Bitch Trilogy' set in 1977.

Characters

HOPE JACKSON, *a teenager*
DESTINY, *her mother*
FRANK, *her father*
HENRY, *her boyfriend*
LUKE, *Frank's brother*
KATIE, *Luke's daughter*
POLICEMAN
REPORTERS
RACE CALLER / RADIO ANNOUNCER *(voice only)*

The action takes place in rural New South Wales.

Scene 1

HOPE*'s bedroom at their property, about 45 km from town.* HOPE *is making preparations for her farewell party and her mother is packing suitcases.*

DESTINY

You're such an ungrateful child Hope. You're just plain bloody selfish. What about me? Didja eva stop ta think? You've been a little bitch to me all you bloomin' life so I don't see why you should change now. In the middle of the shearing! Couldn't you at least have picked a better time? /

HOPE

/I can't help when uni starts Mum I'm not the boss of the world.

DESTINY

Scholarship or no scholarship lassie some things are more important in life. Family. Obligations. Responsibility. The Farm. The farm, lord knows what will happen to the farm what with your father being the biggest bludger in the world and always begging your Uncle Luke for more money and I can't be expected to hold things together forever on my own you know. Selfish. What you'll do, missy, oh I know exactly what you'll do, you'll get to that la-di-da Sydney University place you little tart and you'll root around till your heart's content and then you'll come home anyway and marry poor Henry who's been pining after you like a dog this last summer and all this education rubbish, what good will it do you then? Mathematics teacher my fat arse, you'll have a party for four years, without a care for all my hardships, then come back and you'll be too stuck up to even talk to the stupid hairdresser/

HOPE

/Mum it's a bonded scholarship I won't be coming back I have to go where the Department of Education sends me when I'm finished. I've explained this to you a million times.

DESTINY

And as if that scholarship will be enough. You'll be asking your Uncle

Luke for money left right and bloody centre by the way change of plans Luke's driving you into the pub tonight, your Dad and I will be in later.

At the mention of this change of plans, LUKE *appears in the bedroom, and* HOPE *freezes in her preparations.* DESTINY *can not see him. During the following, he removes his clothes and beckons* HOPE, *who responds.*

DESTINY

Now don't you start. You can't expect Dad to miss the end of the cricket just on account of a silly farewell party. Honestly Hope you think you'd take better care of your things, sew a few buttons on now and again. No one will be taking care of little miss lazy slut in the big smoke will they now? And you'll miss your friends. And your Dad. And Katie, and Uncle Luke. You'll probably never see your Grandma again, what about that? And you'll lose Henry, mark my words.

DESTINY *stops packing and speaks to the audience.* LUKE *and* HOPE *fuck.*

Once upon a time there were two brothers, between them they had the biggest properties in the district. A girl couldn't have done better for herself. It really didn't seem to matter which one I married. Frank was always the talker, but Luke was the stud. Whoahee! The times we had. But I did the right thing, the sensible choice. I was very happy with Frank. I must admit, Vietnam proved to be a bit of a hiccup, in the fidelity stakes, I mean what's a young girl meant to do for a bit a fun when your man's away and all you have for company is a nosy nipper like her? Luke. He was a great help in running the property. He helped me keep all the important machinery well lubricated.

HOPE

[*Still coupling*] Mum. Muuuuum. Mummy.

LUKE *finishes, abandons* HOPE, *exits.*

DESTINY

There are in my opinion far too many obligations in life always pulling you sideways. And some things just aren't what they're cracked up to be. Motherhood, for one.

DESTINY *finishes packing.* HOPE *dresses and applies lipstick.*

DESTINY

There. All packed. Ready to piss off into the wild blue yonder.

HOPE

Thank you. Mother.

DESTINY

Darling, I . . . [*she makes as if to embrace her*]

A knock at the bedroom door, followed by LUKE*'s entry.*

LUKE

Not interrupting anything I hope. How are my girls then?

DESTINY *stares at* HOPE *staring at* LUKE *and realises for the first time.*

LUKE

Are we ready then? Party time!

DESTINY

Just go. Will you both just go.

LUKE

Des. Destiny. Give the girl a break will ya.

DESTINY

And be quick about it.

LUKE

You should be proud of her Des. Be happy for the girl.

DESTINY

Happy?

HOPE

Yeah. Why not. I'll see you soon Mum. Please don't be too late.

LUKE

Come on, the party can't start without ya.

HOPE

Seeya Mum [*a kiss*].

They leave.

DESTINY

Happy my arse.

Scene 2

At the pub in town. A large sign with 'Congratulations and Good luck HOPE*' along with other festive decorations adorn the pub.* HOPE *enters to loud cheers by all.*

ALL

'For she's a jolly good fellow' [*etc*].

After the final cheers, HENRY *goes to* HOPE *with a schooner.*

HENRY

Here's to the best root I've never had.

HOPE

You never know your luck.

HENRY

I'm so proud of you. Good on ya Hope. Hey where's ya oldies.

HOPE

Oh you know Mum's chucking a shitty as usual, Dad's watching the cricket, Luke's gone to pick up Katie. They'll be here soon.

HENRY

Katie's been here for ages doing the decorations. Fact. Drinking too many shandies. Fact. She's all ready passed out in the beer garden. Fact.

HOPE

Well that's where he said he was going. When he dropped me. Fact.

HENRY

Maybe he's gone mad and they had to shoot him.

HOPE

Wouldn't that be nice. [*Skulls beer*] I'm going to check on my matie Katie.

HENRY

Hope . . .

HOPE

Henry.

HENRY

Hope do you remember when we were little.

HOPE

Der!

HENRY

That time at the district swimming carnival?

HENRY *scuttles under a table, meant to be reminiscent of the bleachers at Olympic swimming pools, making a little nest with the towels. The pub crowd turns into spectators.* HOPE *is on the bar, swimming her race.*

RACE CALLER

[*Through megaphone*] And here comes young Hope Jackson from

Condobolin taking over everybody on the last lap of the medley, my, my, freestyle is her strength, look at her pulling ahead, she could catch an emu with a speed on like that and yes, yes, the race is Hope's, and coming in second is Narelle Howard from Cowra and that little whippersnapper from Forbes Lisa Rose a close third. We'll just check those times for you to see if they qualify to go on to State level but what a race, what a great finish, well done girls.

HOPE *grabs her towel as the crowd cheers and congratulates, then makes her way to her hidey hole with* HENRY.

HOPE

Did ya see that?

HENRY

Nope. Knew ya'd win though.

HOPE

Your turn soon. Better win.

HENRY

I might.

HOPE

Then we could go away to Sydney together and never come back.

HENRY

Watcha always talking about running away for?

HOPE

I don't.

HENRY

You do too.

HOPE

I dunno. I like being away.

HENRY

Well we're away now.

HOPE

Just for a day.

HENRY

Hope.

HOPE

Yeah. What.

HENRY

Well, I . . .

HOPE

What!

HENRY

Do ya wanna be my girlfriend?

HOPE

Yeah. Alright.

They kiss.

HENRY

My girlfriend the swimming emu.

HOPE

Do ya wanna root then?

HENRY

What! Here!

HOPE

Why not?

HENRY

Well I gotta swim in a race in a minute you drongo. I don't wanna stand up on the blocks with a stiffy.

HOPE

Yeah. S'pose.

HENRY

I like you better than anything Hope Jackson. And on Saturday night I'm going take you down to the dam and we'll catch yabbies and cook them and watch the shooting stars.

They kiss. KATIE *enters calling out for* HOPE. *The scene returns to present and the party at the pub.*

KATIE

Hope! Hope Jackson where are you! Get over here.

HOPE *approaches* KATIE.

KATIE

I need to talk to you.

KATIE *pulls* HOPE *roughly outside just as the policeman enters.*

POLICEMAN

Anyone tell me where young Hope Jackson is please?

Scene 3

Flashback to an earlier time. HOPE *and* FRANK *are watching the cricket on television, the sound track of a 70s match could run in the background. Conversation flows around the action of the match.*

FRANK

Done your homework love?

HOPE

Daddy, it's the holidays you duffa.

FRANK

Yeah. So it is.

He goes to window and looks out.

FRANK

Fucking wind. Good for fucking nothing.

HOPE

Dad.

FRANK

Yeah.

Silence

FRANK

[*Still looking at the wind*] What is it love?

Silence

FRANK

Everything OK at school last term?

HOPE

'Course.

FRANK

Yeah. Bloody little smartarse aren't you! You show 'em darlin', show those stuck up teachers a thing a two. Bloody teachers, been at bloody school all their life, what do they know about anything.

HOPE

Dad, they're not all wallies.

FRANK

Rubbish. Wankers and draft dodgers, the lot of 'em.

They watch cricket.

FRANK

You'll go a long way sweetheart.

More cricket.

FRANK

Just you wait and see sweetheart.

HOPE

Yeah.

FRANK

Yeah.

HOPE

I guess I might.

FRANK

[*To TV*] Bloody poofters those Poms, the bloody lot of them.

HOPE

Maybe I'll go to England. You know. After I finish school and university and everything.

FRANK

Don't be bloody stupid love, pass us the tele guide will ya?

Silence. Cricket.

FRANK

What'ya wanna do something like that for sweetheart? Honestly Hope, take a good look at what you'd be letting yourself in for. Look at 'em [*points at TV*]. Hardly good breeding stock are they?

HOPE

S'pose not.

Silence. Cricket.

FRANK

Not much choice 'round here when you think about it though, is there love?

Silence. Cricket.

FRANK

Don't worry darling. Henry'll ask you out again.

HOPE

Dad!

FRANK

Mark my words. Best looking girl west of the ranges, you are.

She laughs at his teasing as he reaches over and tussles her hair.

FRANK

Cheer up love. We're winning the cricket.

HOPE

Yeah.

FRANK

Yeah.

HOPE

Dad.

FRANK

It's alright darling. You can go wherever you want. Your Mum and me can manage the farm on our own. Well, your bloody mother can, I'm sure.

HOPE

I really want to go to uni next year Dad. University. In Sydney.

FRANK

Good idea sweetheart.

TOGETHER

Howzat!!!!!!

FRANK

Howzbloody that! Best catch all day.

DESTINY

[*Off*] Will you two keep it down in there, I am trying to talk to your brother on the phone. Business. Work, Frank, in case you can remember what that is.

FRANK

[*Loudly to* DESTINY] Stuff my bloody brother and why isn't he watching the cricket anyway? [*To* HOPE] Luke. Oooooerrrr [*pulls face*].

HOPE

[*Laughs*] Dad!

Silence. Cricket.

FRANK

You flap your little wings and fly away sweetheart.

Cricket. HOPE *speaks to the audience now.*

HOPE

My father made me feel like an angel, with wings bigger than Kosciusko, so strong I could traverse the universe. He made me believe that anything was possible. That I was safe. Well. That part's a lie. [*Pause*] Do you think he knew?

Silence

FRANK

[*Goes to window again*] Fucking wind.

Scene 4

Also an earlier time. HENRY *and* LUKE *and* FRANK *in the kitchen, drinking tea, watching* DESTINY *make scones.*

DESTINY

She should be home any minute. I hope she's not in a foul mood because she didn't win. I hope. God all I want is a good lay down.

DESTINY *puts the scones in the oven and stands staring out the kitchen door, smoking. The men speak at the same time, choral-like and in unison where bold indicates.*

FRANK

[*Singing*] 'Lay down lay down, lay down, lay it all down, let your white dadeedee-daa laa dee dee we were so close there was no room we bled inside each other's wounds we all had caught the same disease we all sang the songs of peace/ lay down lay down lay it all down yeah yeah yeah yeah yeah so raise the candles high cause if we do you know we could sat black against the sky

LUKE

/Of course, I'll go straight to hell. But I'm not a monster you know. I waited as long as I could. I fucked Destiny as long as any man could stand too. I waited and waited and waited and waited. She unfolded like an angel's wings, right before my eyes. Budding. Hope. There is no other name for a woman like that. Hope. That is what she gave me. You know my wife

HENRY

/Next year, at Hope's farewell party, I'll ask her to marry me, and she'll say no. She'll tell me to marry Katie, who incidentally I lost my virginity with because well, Hope is too good to practice on. If I had to drive forever in my ute, like if that is what God decided I had to do in this life, just drive, then Hope is the only passenger I want. Ever. /I know her Dad's a psycho

and raise them higher again then if you do we could stay dry against the rain lay down lay down lay/ it all down dadeeddeedaad dda-aa some came to sing some came to pray same came to keep the dark away you gotta lay down, lay down, you gotta lay down, lay it on down so raise the candles high cause if we do you know we could sat black against the sky and raise them higher again then if you do we could stay dry against the rain, you gotta lay down, lay down, lay it all down.' As far as I can tell, I killed more men than women or children in Vietnam. /I can't tell you how happy I am that Hope is free from the blight of Communism. /She'll be my only gift in this life. Or any other. Because I am a lost man. And she's going to leave me.

wouldn't let me touch her, not after the fourth miscarriage. And Destiny, well she moaned a huge hole in my heart. After the first time I touched Hope/ I went home and couldn't sleep then went out to the empty shearer's huts and tried to get up the courage to blow my head off. /But I thought, if I do this, I'll never see her again, never be able to say sorry. /She'll be my only gift in this life. Or any other. Because I am a bad man. And she's going to leave me.

and her Uncle's a perv. And her Mum, well, Des is what I suppose you'd call a bitter woman. But me, I take better care of my crops. I'm planning to name a potato after Hope. /She'll be my only gift in this life. Or any other. Because I am a stupid man. And she's going to leave me.

Silence. More tea is poured. DESTINY *smokes.*

DESTINY

You know, you blokes are so full of shit sometimes. [*Still staring at the endless paddocks*] Maybe Hope should get out of here. Who can feel at home in this god forsaken place? Whose bloody land is it anyway? If you ask me it wasn't worth putting no arsenic in the flour over.

Silence

FRANK

Those scones are burning Des.

DESTINY

Is that so Frank? [*She saves the scones*]

FRANK

[*Going to the back door*] That'll be the dust from the school bus.

DESTINY

Rightio. She'll be here in ten minutes. Smiles on boys.

Scene 5

The present. HOPE *is at the police station being questioned.*

SARGEANT

Right. Hope love. Now I'm sorry to spoil your party with . . . with this bad news about your Uncle's death. I'm sorry I had to drag you in here. But you were the last person to see him alive and well, let's face it love, it looks pretty damn suspicious.

HOPE

Sarge, I/really want to tell . . .

SARGEANT

/Now look here love, I'm the one who names the criminals in this town. Now pay attention to me because I'm only going to say this once. Before I ask the others in. I'm going to give you the best piece of advice you'll ever get in your life now and I want you to promise me to follow it. Just say no. You did not kill him. Do you hear me Hope?

RADIO ANNOUNCER

We interrupt the cricket to bring you news just to hand, an update on the murder victim found early this evening. The body has now been identified as that of local farmer and businessman, Luke Jackson. Rotarian and former Mayor, it is presumed that Mr Jackson was murdered en route to a social event. Police are asking for anyone who may have seen any suspicious travellers in the district, or with any information at all, to come forward. Mr Jackson is survived by his wife and daughter. Back to the cricket.

HOPE

I...

SARGEANT

You don't have to thank me love.

HOPE

But...

SARGEANT

There's more people who know more things around here than you think young lady.

The REPORTERS *arrive.*

HOPE

I'm really sorry.

SARGEANT

Run along now Hope. Drop me a line when you're rich and famous.

HOPE *leaves.*

SARGEANT

Yes, it is true, Hope Jackson was the last to see him alive.

REPORTER

And she arrived at the pub driving his car?

SARGEANT

That is correct.

REPORTER

How can you explain that sarge?

SARGEANT

Our inquiries have convinced us that Hope was driving her Uncle's car because he was drunk. During the journey Luke Jackson insulted Hope's mother, his sister-in-law, a fight ensued, he asked to be let out of the car, and Hope left him on the highway, very close to where his body was found.

REPORTER

And the cause of death?

SARGEANT

Well the poor bloke's still got to have an autopsy, but the Doctor suspects it was a brain haemorrhage resulting from a severe knock on the head, probably from falling off the bridge onto the rocks below. Shame about the drought, if there'd been any water in that creek he might still be alive. Right. Wrap it up folks. That's it for tonight.

REPORTER

But Sarge/what about if he was pushed, I mean how can you . . .

SARGEANT

/Now you listen to me matey. I've been a policeman out here in the bush for thirty-two bloody long years and I've seen all kinds of things. I know an accident when I see one. Now piss off the lot of yas before I really lose my temper.

They leave. The SARGEANT *rips up some papers.*

SARGEANT

You poor little lamb Hope.

Scene 6

Earlier that evening, back at the pub. KATIE *is outside in the beergarden with* HOPE.

KATIE

I saw you.

HOPE

What.

KATIE

With him.

Silence

KATIE

My Dad.

Silence

HOPE

Him. Did you?

Pause

KATIE

Things were different once weren't they?

HOPE

Were they?

KATIE

When we were little. They were.

Flashback to a backyard barbecue at dusk, the girls are now small children. Uncles and Aunties and others flood the stage in revelry.

KATIE

I am having such a really truly good time.

HOPE

Yeah me too.

KATIE

I hope they forget we're still awake!

HOPE

Yeah! We can stay up all night!

KATIE

Go down to the river! And . . .

HOPE & KATIE

Go around to Henry's and throw rocks at his window!

KATIE

They'll never find us here those other kids.

HOPE

Nah you're right. Jeez they're slack.

KATIE

Too little to play hide'n'seek properly.

HOPE

Betch ya they've given up.

KATIE

Let's go see.

HOPE

Yeah OK.

They run around wildly chasing kids. KATIE *begins counting to one hundred and* HOPE *hides.* LUKE *slips away and follows* HOPE *to her hiding spot.*

LUKE

Boo!

HOPE *squeals.*

LUKE

Don't squeal honey they'll find you. Anyway. You're too big for this game. You don't really like it do you?

HOPE

Sometimes. Yeah.

LUKE

Want to play a game with me instead?

HOPE

No.

She goes to run away but LUKE *grabs her.*

LUKE

Game's over darlin'.

They walk off into the darkness. HOPE *willingly takes his hand when he offers it.* KATIE *calls out* HOPE*'s name again and again.*

KATIE

Hope. Hope. Hope.

Back in the present.

KATIE

Hope. It's OK. I don't care what happened.

Silence

KATIE

I saw everything you know.

As KATIE *relates the following story,* HOPE *re-enacts the scene with* LUKE.

KATIE

'Cause I was there. Waiting for Sparky to pick me up. When I saw you coming down the track I hid, I mean you know what Dad thinks of bloody Sparky. And you stopped the car and Dad got out to check the mail, and when he turned around you were already on the roof with his shotgun. I thought you were going to shoot his fucking head off I swear. But no. You just thwacked him good and hard. On the head. A few too many times I thought. And you kept saying . . .

KATIE AND HOPE

Stop it. Stop it.

KATIE

Stop it you filthy fucker. Well he was. And then you drove off.

HOPE

I couldn't stop myself.

KATIE

I had time to drag him over to the bridge and shove him off before Sparky arrived. God that boy is unreliable. Five o'clock, he swore black and blue he wouldn't keep me waiting. Bloody cricket.

Silence

KATIE

Please don't go away.

Scene 7

The local train station the next morning. HOPE *is sitting alone on the platform.* HENRY *appears.*

HENRY

Please don't go Hope.

HOPE

Not you too Henry.

HENRY

Me too what?

HOPE

I sometimes thought that . . . well, that you were the only one on my side. About leaving.

HENRY

I am. On your side.

HOPE

Henry.

HENRY

We could get married you know. Shit. That was romantic wasn't it.

HOPE

Oh Henry.

She kisses him goodbye. HENRY *leaves. Silence.* DESTINY *arrives. She walks up the long platform and drapes a large warm coat around* HOPE*'s shoulder.*

DESTINY

You'll be needing this sweetheart. Take care.

HOPE

Where's Dad?

DESTINY

He's . . . he's a bit gone Sweetheart. I guess we all are. I'm sorry.

Sound of approaching train. DESTINY *leaves.* HOPE *remains alone on the platform as the train approaches.*

THE END

Unbidden

This is the second play in 'The Bitch Trilogy' set in 1988.

Characters

HOPE, *in her late 20s*
HENRY, *the same, her childhood sweetheart*
KATIE, *her cousin and best friend*
JULIAN, *Hope's English boyfriend*
DESTINY, *Hope's mother (dead)*
FRANK, *Hope's father (dead)*
LUKE, *Hope's Uncle (dead)*
PRIEST
SHEARERS
THERAPIST

Scene 1

The back paddock on HENRY*'s farm.* JULIAN, HENRY *and the* PRIEST *are waiting underneath a tree by the river, dressed in tuxedos. The* PRIEST *is wearing cowboy boots.*

JULIAN

This is really spiritual. [*Silence*] Who would ever want to get married in a church in England after this experience. [*Silence*] And this idea of a private ceremony at dusk under the tree you proposed, that's deeply real. [*Silence*] Not too many people to ruin the ambience, a quiet picnic afterwards to honour the ceremony rather than worship the grape and hops excessively as you're wont to in this vast brown land. [*Silence*] A simple ritual and a grand moment. [*Silence*] I still think however that you should have allowed me to play my didgeridoo.

HENRY *and the* PRIEST

Shut up Julian.

HENRY

You're a right bloody drongo when you want to be mate.

JULIAN

Right. Right you are. Sorry chaps.

JULIAN *begins to hum imitating a didgeridoo. He then brings one out from behind the tree and attempts to play.*

HENRY

Christ where are those women. Sorry Father.

PRIEST

I believe that's them now.

KATIE *and* HOPE *arrive driving a tractor. They circle the men, stop, alight.* KATIE *is clearly pregnant and they are both a bit drunk.*

HOPE

How about that heat eh?

KATIE

I do.

PRIEST

I think I get to speak first Katie, from memory.

KATIE

Oh Henry darling I love you.

HENRY

And I love you Katie.

They kiss.

HOPE

And I love you both.

HOPE *takes* HENRY *out of* KATIE*'s arms and kisses him passionately.* JULIAN *gets overexcited about his didgeridoo playing and attempts a tribal dance as well.*

ALL

Julian!

He stops.

PRIEST

Ahem. Let's get this show on the road then.

JULIAN

Hope I was just thinking about our lovely house on the square and our little tennis court in the garden and London in the spring, and how long it is since we've been to Covent Garden for a decent coffee let alone the opera and then I suddenly realised you're absolutely right. We should stay. We should 'go bush' as you put it. Live here. Forever.

KATIE

She's already lived here longer than forever Julian, you wally. I think she's had enough of it, don't you?

The tractor suddenly starts rolling. HENRY *and* HOPE *bolt after it and* HOPE *jumps up and manages to put the brake on. She jumps down into his arms. They embrace awkwardly.*

HOPE

The thing is Henry . . .

KATIE

[*Stomping her feet*] Henry Henry Henry I'm pregnant.

HOPE

. . . I just can't.

They break away and return to their rightful partners.

HENRY

I know Katie. I know.

HOPE

Just fucking marry her. For once and all.

JULIAN

Hope.

KATIE

Here here.

HENRY

Katie.

KATIE

Hope Jackson you're a greedy greedy woman.

JULIAN

[*Abandoning didgeridoo*] I just don't understand you Hope. Sometimes. I swear . . .

Sounds of a hundred kookaburras. The priest begins the rights. JULIAN *holds* HOPE, *who cries throughout the short ceremony.*

HOPE

Take me home Julian. Please.

Sounds of the bush flood the stage, soon to be overwhelmed by urban sirens.

Scene 2

Before. HOPE *is collecting eggs from the chook pen. She revels in their beauty. She locks the temperamental gate and struggles with the egg basket and her suitcase—which looks really out of place on the dusty farm, as do the smart clothes she is wearing—and walks over to the farm house. She places her suitcase next to the coffin, which she does not notice, and sits fondling the eggs for a while. Presently she gets up and begins to repeatedly open and close the screen door, hypnotised by its squeak. Finally she goes inside with the eggs.*

HOPE

Mum, Dad, where are you?

HOPE *goes outside again and oils the door. She begins throwing eggs at the corrugated iron fence of the chook pen.*

HOPE

He loves me. [*Splat*] He loves me not. [*Splat*] He loves me, [*splat*] He loves me not . . .

The coffin lid opens, HOPE*'s parent's climb out to meet her.*

DESTINY

Hope. You're back.

FRANK

Don't waste the eggs darling. The bloody chooks have just started laying again.

HOPE *continues to throw eggs. She cannot hear her parents.*

FRANK

Hope. Hope. Hope! Stop that sweetheart.

DESTINY

Ah leave her alone Frank. She came didn't she? Give her a break.

FRANK

You've changed your tune.

DESTINY

Yeah. 'Spose. Better late than never.

FRANK

Too right.

DESTINY

Too late, more likely.

HOPE *stops throwing eggs. She moves to the coffin, closing the lid.*

HOPE

'Hi Hope, How are ya? Long time no see! So, how's things been in London town? Bit of a big shot now, aren't ya! That's my little nipper, show them poms a thing or too about . . . what is it exactly that you do sweetheart?' Oh lordy lordy I've been back quarter of an hour and I'm already talking to myself.

FRANK

Go on Des, have a word with her.

DESTINY

Leave her be.

FRANK

Go on.

DESTINY

Frank I know I've always made my excuses with Hope ever since she was a little one, but this time I feel . . . Oh for Christ's sake Frank wake up to yourself will ya we're dead.

FRANK

Yeah. Yeah. Guess we are.

DESTINY

A bit too late to ask . . . .

They circle HOPE *with their questions.*

FRANK

Why did you have to leave Hope? I mean I understand about running off to uni and all, but what about the holidays eh? You never came home once, and then you pissed off to London.

DESTINY

Before the graduation ceremony even. So tell me Hope, about you and Luke. Word is around here/

FRANK

/Nobody talks about it anymore darling so why didn't you ever come home and see your good old Dad?

DESTINY

Word is that you and him, well, it's rubbish isn't it! He was your Uncle. Besides . . .

FRANK

He was your piece of fluff wasn't he Des? My brother.

DESTINY

Don't start Frank. I'm warning you.

FRANK

Don't start my arse.

DESTINY

My arse my arse! I mean it.

FRANK

No Des. I was the one who meant it.

They cease. All relax on the verandah.

FRANK

Just be nice for once in your life.

DESTINY

I'm out of practice.

FRANK

Well Hope. How are things in London darling? Everything alright? Your mum and me we miss you something fierce you know.

HOPE

They never knew anything about me. After I left. Like, my suntan fades and I disappeared from their landscape. A few lousy phone calls then nothing. Zilch.

DESTINY

Hello. Hello Hope. You sound like you're in the next room. Yeah, yeah, the shearing's going fine. So. What's your week been like?

HOPE *lies down after stripping down to her underwear and slips on a hospital gown. She is undergoing an abortion with a local anaesthetic. She speaks to the audience.*

HOPE

I really like London. It's so . . . full of surprises. And romance. Last week was a riot. I was in this hospital. 'My colleague' she said, of rubber gloved queen, 'would like to observe the proceedings, I trust you have no objections.' Giggle snort. 'We all have to learn some time!' Ha ha. And then a bloody med student who looked about twelve years old scraped my baby away. French mud, French blood, going down backwards in an English drainpipe. Oh he was such a nice boy Mum. He never phoned me either.

She rolls over and sleeps.

DESTINY

That'll teach her. To screw around with foreigners.

FRANK

Well. We'd better be off or they'll run out of beer before we get there.

FRANK *exits. Flashback to when they were newly married.*

DESTINY

Nothing beats a Saturday night in the bush.

DESTINY *applies some lipstick and prepares to leave. Some music from the Saturday night dance beckons in the background.*

DESTINY

Coming Frank. You start up the ute.

She fixes a smile, picks up a pavlova from the outside freezer on the verandah and makes to exit. She sees HOPE *asleep and is jolted back to the present. She removes her 1950s party dress.* HOPE *wakes as* DESTINY *begins her story.* DESTINY *undresses down to her underwear whilst talking.* HOPE *also takes her hospital gown off.*

DESTINY

I felt so emancipated when I decided. After watching your husband fall asleep night after night after you've fed it seemed like thousands of shearers three meals a day, a million days a year and were hoping for a bit of company, but he was even too tired to smile at you over dinner, the decision comes easy. So when he's snoring, you kiss him gently, because by God you love him. Then you sneak outside in your knickers and his undone shirt around you, with the wind licking your nipples, and the pink peppercorns popping under your feet, meeting your secret man on the riverbank.

DESTINY & HOPE

[*Whispering*] Sex, sex, sex, sex, sex, sex, sex, sex, sex, seeeexxxxxx.

DESTINY

I could have drowned on those nights and been a happy woman, it was so good. Just/

DESTINY & HOPE

[*whispering in a chant*] /me and him and the water. And the stars in the sky. That's all I need to get me by.

DESTINY

All my life my cottontails have been caked with mud or blood.

Both women confront each other in their state of undress. HOPE *pulls some clothes back on.* DESTINY *grabs her coat, and tucks* HOPE*'s hair behind her ears before leaving.*

HOPE

Goodbye Mum.

DESTINY

Goodbye Hope Darlin'. Take care.

Sound of ute starting up. DESTINY *exits. Sound of car leaving. Dust.*

HOPE

Goodbye Dad.

HOPE *closes the lid of the coffin. She telephones.*

HOPE

Henry? Hi, it's me. I'm home. Yeah. Bit late, but I made it.

Scene 3

The present. HENRY *and* HOPE *at* HOPE*'s place. They're drinking on the verandah.*

HENRY
What's he like then this pommy bloke of yours?

HOPE
Nothing like you that's for sure.

HENRY
Thanks.

HOPE
No worries.

Silence

HOPE
So when're you getting married then.

HENRY
Me and Katie?

HOPE
No you and me you drongo. Of course you and Katie.

HENRY
Oh you know.

HOPE
Jesus Henry.

HENRY
Soon. We're not having a big bash. Under the circumstances.

HOPE

Just as long as I'm invited.

HENRY

Course you are.

HOPE

Someone's gotta make sure you go through with it. Shotgun wedding and all.

HENRY

Yeah. Right.

HOPE

Don't look so gloomy Hen. Wedded bliss awaits you.

HENRY

Geezus.

Flashback. FRANK *and* DESTINY *are in their bedroom.* FRANK *hits* DESTINY.

DESTINY

Frank. Stop. I don't want to discuss this now. We have guests arriving in half an hour, and I still have to put my face on. So just piss off will ya.

FRANK

Why Des? Why?

DESTINY

You knew what kind of girl I was when you married me Frank. And he'll be gone as soon as the shearing's done.

FRANK *breaks down.*

DESTINY

You're an irate bastard but I love you Frank. You know that. I will never forget what you did for me. Or every thing you've been through. And one day Hope will marry some bloke and she'll come home and they'll take over the farm and look after us when we're old and batty. Too old to even remember what sex was. Now go on, get out of my light. I need to put my lippy on.

FRANK *leaves.* DESTINY *freezes. Sound of two gunshots. Back to present.*

HENRY

Too many gun licenses in the country really. When you think about it.

HOPE

Thanks for cleaning up Henry.

Scene 4

On the riverbank at the farm. HENRY *and* HOPE *are in the water.* KATIE *and* JULIAN *are tending to the barbecue.*

KATIE

You're not half as bad as I thought you'd be you know.

JULIAN

Thank God for that. What on earth did you think I'd be?

KATIE

Posh. Condescending. Whinging about the heat all the time.

JULIAN

Well, I do do a bit of that.

KATIE

Strewth don't we all.

JULIAN

Well you're not either. Like I thought you'd be.

KATIE

No?

JULIAN

No.

KATIE

Prettier am I?

JULIAN

Indeed.

KATIE

[*Yelling*] Come on you two the bangers are getting burnt.

JULIAN

Quieter too.

KATIE

Smartarse.

JULIAN

And so poetic.

KATIE

Just butter the bread matie. You shoulda quit while you were ahead.

JULIAN

Sage as well.

KATIE

Stop flirting. I'm an engaged woman I'll have you know.

JULIAN

Yes. Congratulations.

HOPE *and* HENRY *join* KATIE *and* JULIAN.

HENRY

What for?

KATIE

For being engaged you big dickhead in case you've forgotten. So. How about you two. Any wedding plans.

HENRY

Katie.

HOPE

Well . . .

JULIAN

Go on sweetheart spill the beans.

HOPE

Not exactly wedding plans but . . . we've been thinking about staying.

KATIE

What?!

HOPE

Moving back. Dropping out. Freelancing. Whatever you call it.

JULIAN

I've never been keen to bring the children up in London.

HENRY

What children?

JULIAN

Our future progeny.

HOPE

I miss it. I miss home.

KATIE

I am completely gobsmacked. Gobsmacked.

KATIE *runs down to the river and pulls out the wine that has been cooling there.*

KATIE

Let's get pissed!

JULIAN

Jolly good idea.

JULIAN *goes to find some glasses.*

HENRY

'Jolly good idea'. Geezus.

HOPE

Whad'ya reckon Hen?

HENRY

Pricktease.

HOPE

Don't Hen. Please don't.

Silence

HENRY

Someone's has to run the joint I s'pose. Hate to see a good property go under.

Scene 4

Before. London. HOPE*'s therapist's office. Throughout the scene the ghost of* LUKE *lingers.*

HOPE

He's been dead for more than ten years now. I mean, how long is this going to take? Will I still be dealing with this until the day I die? You know that's what gets to me the most about this whole thing, this whole fucking scenario, that it just won't go away.

THERAPIST

Mmmm.

HOPE

And I can't ever go back there. Not with everyone knowing. I can't deal with the control he still has over the way I live my life. I just can't stand it anymore.

THERAPIST

Hope. Listen close now. Has it ever crossed your mind that you might be telling some lies? That if you spoke the truth, then you'd be giving yourself something to deal with. And that then you might be able to move on. Make some real progress.

HOPE

What do you mean?

THERAPIST

Come on Hope. You slept with the man for seven years.

HOPE

He raped me. [*Silence*] How dare you.

THERAPIST

Every single time for seven long years even when you were a grown women with enough intelligence to extract yourself from the situation? Come on Hope. You liked it. You liked him. [*Silence*] Precisely what are you ashamed of here?

Scene 5

After. Shearing shed on HOPE*'s property. A party is in full swing.*

RINGER

So in closing Julian we feel obliged to warn you not to mess with Aussie sheilas, especially Miss Hope here, who's got a mighty reputation for getting rid of fellas who piss her off. For good. So behave yourself. And congratulations. To the Bride and Groom!

ALL

The Bride and Groom.

RINGER

And if you'll allow me to break with tradition, I'd like to propose another toast. As youse all know, I've worked on the Jackson property for more seasons than I can remember. I taught that beautiful looking woman over there in the white frock how to shear a sheep before she'd even kissed her first boy. And we all missed her when she went away to school, and college and fuck knows what we did to piss her off enough to run away to England. But she came home. And it hasn't been easy. Not very nice circumstances. We're all sad about Mr and Mrs Jackson, especially not having them here today, and by cripes they loved a party those two. But I just want to say we're all happy to have you back home Hope. And you can boss me around whenever you like. Get used to it Julian! So here's to the boss and her hubby.

ALL

The boss and her hubby!

RINGER

Now fill up yer glasses and put your hands together for Mackie and Johnno who've got a bit of entertainment for you by way of a wedding present.

Applause. The two shearers take centre stage, singing 'Click go the shears'.

MACKIE

No seriously folks. We don't mean to bore you. We just wanted to give Hope and Julian their present but we didn't know how to wrap it.

JOHNNO

Yeah well you can't can you, because its

MACKIE

It's not something you can put paper around it's

JOHNNO

It's a change in attitude

MACKIE

Yeah. Manners. We've got some new manners in the shed, on account of having a woman boss with a posh pommie husband.

JOHNNO

Yeah we thought we'd better scrub up our act

MACKIE

and we started with our language so here it is. Our wedding present for Hope and Julian. The Offical New Language Policy of the Jackson Shed.

JOHNNO

It goes like this.

MACKIE

Yeah and from Monday the notice'll be stuck up here in the shed and anyone who breaks the rules will be out on their ear.

JOHNNO

Too right. So whereas before you might hear a bloke saying 'No fucking way', he now will be requested to mind his language and say something like

MACKIE

'I'm fairly sure that's not feasible' instead.

JOHNNO

And so on. 'You're fucking kidding' becomes

MACKIE

Really.

JOHNNO

'Tell someone who gives a fuck'.

MACKIE

Have you run that by the boss?

JOHNNO

'No cunt told me'.

MACKIE

I wasn't involved in that conversation.

JOHNNO

'Eat shit and die'.

MACKIE

Is that so?

JOHNNO

'Eat shit and die motherfucker'.

MACKIE

Is that so, Sir?

JOHNNO

'He's a fucken prick'.

MACKIE

He's somewhat insensitive.

JOHNNO
'You haven't got a fucken clue'.

MACKIE
You need to consider this some more.

JOHNNO
'Fuck off shithead'.

MACKIE
Well there you go.

JOHNNO
'You're a fucken wanker'.

MACKIE
You're the boss's husband and I respect you.

JOHNNO
'This place is fucked'.

MACKIE
We're a little disorganised in the Jackson shed today.

JOHNNO
'What sort of a fuckwit are you?'

MACKIE
You're new here aren't you?

JOHNNO
'You are fucking paranoid.'

MACKIE
Are you from England?

JOHNNO
'You are fucking useless.'

MACKIE

Are you from New Zealand?

JOHNNO

'Fuck off.'

MACKIE

I'll look into it and get back to you.

JOHNNO

'Fuck off dickhead.'

MACKIE

I no longer require your assistance.

JOHNNO

'You fucking loser.'

MACKIE

Gee, that was unfortunate.

JOHNNO

So ladies and gentlemen you get the general idea. No more fucking swearing. There's a lady present. And aint we all pleased about that.

MACKIE

To Julian and Hope, may your life together be long and happy!

ALL

To Julian and Hope!

Cheers. Music. JULIAN *and* HOPE *kiss to more cheers.* KATIE *steals* JULIAN *for a dance, and* HENRY *takes* HOPE *outside. He kisses her.*

HENRY

Welcome home. Hope Jackson. Welcome back to the world of the living.

HOPE sees a figure in the shadows. It is LUKE's ghost. She turns her back on it. He disappears.

HOPE

Thank you Henry. Thank you.

The night darkens and a thousand stars fill the sky.

THE END

Perpetual

This is the third play of 'The Bitch trilogy', set in 1999.

Characters

HOPE, *now in her 30s*
HENRY, *Hope's childhood sweetheart and friend*
DOCTOR
LUKE, *Hope's uncle (dead)*
KATIE, *Hope's cousin and Henry's wife*
NURSE
DESTINY, *Hope's mother (dead)*
VOICES *of surf club members/beach inspectors*
LONDON TAXI DRIVER
SECRETARY
MASSEUR
BUSINESS PEOPLE / FRIENDS
FRANK, *Hope's father (dead)*

Scene 1

London. HOPE *is in a taxi.*

CABBIE

Been to the theatre then?

HOPE

I suppose so.

CABBIE

Good was it?

HOPE

I suppose.

CABBIE

So where abouts are you from then, in Australia?

HOPE

I can't remember. The Bush.

CABBIE

Been here a while I take it?

HOPE

Long enough.

CABBIE

You Aussies. Bit pushy aren't you, your lot.

HOPE

Pardon?

CABBIE

I mean, we sent you out in irons and a few hundred years later you're still knocking on our door trying to get back in. Cheeky lot.

HOPE

Yeah. I suppose we are.

CABBIE

My brother, he up and went to Brisbane last year, took the whole family. Immigrated.

HOPE

Really.

CABBIE

Yeah. Can't figure it out really.

HOPE

Brisbane is an unexplainable choice, I agree.

CABBIE

Mind you, it's not such a bad idea. The schools in London aren't what they used to be. Got any little ones yourself?

HOPE

No.

CABBIE

Right. Hospitals are going down the gurgler as well. Bloody Labour Government and all.

Silence. Traffic jam. Rain.

CABBIE

So is it our lovely English weather or the London traffic that keeps you here then?

HOPE *laughs.*

HOPE

I can't remember. Not for the life of me.

Scene 2

Later. Sydney. A doctor's surgery.

HENRY

Are you certain? Are you absolutely certain? I mean, how can you be sure? Well, let me tell you something right now, we're getting a second opinion. And a third. It's just a tiny little lump for christsakes. It's tiny. Tiny. It is smaller than a bloody pea. A pea. It's just a pea.

HOPE

Henry . . .

HENRY

Finally. After almost twenty bloody years. You come home. Without your shit-for-brains husband this time. Do not think for one moment Hope Jackson that you have permission to have cancer. I will not allow it. I forbid it. Forbid. Forbid.

HOPE

Henry. It's too late.

DOCTOR

Hope. Henry. I am sorry to have had to tell you this bad news. I can't imagine how you must be feeling. But now that I've been honest with you, we can afford to focus on the positive. Make some decisions. Some plans. We'll know more for sure after the/operation about how widespread it is.

HENRY

/You're going to cut her bloody breasts off and then tell me she's going to die anyway? Aren't you?

DOCTOR

Henry, please, I realise you're upset. Look, how about some tea before we go on? Perhaps you'd like a few moments together before we continue.

HENRY

Why don't you stick your tea right up your . . . your bum and just piss off.

DOCTOR

I'll be back in five minutes. Hope?

HOPE *nods.* DOCTOR *exits.*

HENRY

I'm sorry love. I'm so sorry.

HOPE

Me too.

HOPE *goes to the window that catches her reflection. She unbuttons her blouse and looks at her breasts.* HENRY *comes to her, and embraces her from behind.*

HENRY

Let's go home.

Scene 3

London. Before. HOPE *is at her office. A* MASSEUR *is setting up a workspace.*

SECRETARY

Well. Basically that's it. They said they'd prefer to have someone English running their affairs.

HOPE

English.

SECRETARY

Yes.

HOPE

Reassuring to know Australia isn't the only racist country left in the world.

SECRETARY

So shall I hand their portfolio over to . . . ?

HOPE

Just give it to that new boy down from Oxford. I'm sure he can deal with it.

SECRETARY

Hope. He's about three.

HOPE

At least he's not a colonial.

SECRETARY

I see. OK.

HOPE

What else?

SECRETARY

The usual.

HOPE *strips to her underpants, her secretary hanging her clothes as she does. She lies beneath a towel on a table, being massaged, while her secretary runs through her schedule.*

SECRETARY

If you're willing to speak after the dinner they'd really appreciate it, that's the one at the Savoy next Tuesday. You've got a thank you letter from the charity director acknowledging the donation, and a request from another to sponsor a conference. New York wants to know about next week's meeting, and you still have to get back to Sir Alastair about his invitation for the weekend. So. Aside from Brussels tomorrow there's two more breakfasts and two more lunches to look forward to, one of course being the Board on Friday. Phillipa's phoned twice this morning and said to say that if you stand her up tonight they'll never speak to you again, and to remind you that Godmothers normally do attend birthday parties, in case you didn't know. And they still live in Chelsea, in case you've forgotten. Around the corner, she said to say, from you. Right. You've got to be in Harley Street in 40 minutes Hope or you'll miss the doctor again. Oh. And he rang. Wants to know why you haven't returned his call. And said he's back Friday and he'll meet you Friday night at Waterloo at 7.15 outside the Eurostar terminal.

HOPE

Stop.

SECRETARY

There's a turn up for the books, you going out with him again. I thought it was over between you and Julian?

MASSEUR

Hope. You must try to relax.

HOPE

No. Stop. Please. I've had enough.

HOPE *wraps the towel around her and leaves the table.*

HOPE

Do you know, I bought five pairs of shoes this morning. [*To* MASSEUR] Thank you.

MASSEUR

You need to let me finish with you. Hope?

HOPE

No. No. Thank you.

SECRETARY

What is it Hope?

HOPE

Get me on a plane to Sydney will you?

SECRETARY

What, now?

MASSEUR

Back on the table please.

HOPE

Five pairs.

Scene 4

Now. Sydney. HOPE *and* HENRY *are in bed, in a motel close to the beach.*

HOPE

Do you know Henry I think I got breast cancer because I'm a slut.

HENRY

That's very catholic of you Hope.

HOPE

I am. Being punished for my sins.

HENRY

It's your hobby. Being guilty. Eh.

HOPE

Bastard.

HENRY

Slut.

HOPE

You know what I mean though Henry. There's been too many dirty hands on these breasts.

The telephone rings.

HOPE

Oh Henry, his touch is so long.

HENRY

Let it go sweetheart. He's long dead. Ah bugger.

Answers phone.

HENRY

Yes. Jesus no. No. No. Thank you. Yes. Do that. I'm coming.

HENRY *dresses.*

HENRY

Look darl' there's something I've gotta sort out. Downstairs. I'll be right back.

HOPE

Henry!

HENRY

Sorry love.

HENRY *exits.* HOPE *lights a cigarette.*

HOPE

'I'll be right back'. 'Sorry love'. Bloody men. Bloody Australian men, bloody wankers. God. What have I done.

A large shadow invades the room. A figure of a man soon appears perched on the window. HOPE *yells at the door through which* HENRY *exited.*

HOPE

We are on holiday. You prick. I don't know about you 'sweetheart' but I've been saving up for this for, oh, about two decades! Me and my flat tummy. [*Pause*] Come back here Henry. Henry. My breasts are leaving soon!

The cigarette burns her fingers.

HOPE

Fuckittyfuck. Ow.

HOPE *sucks her finger. The ghost of Uncle* LUKE *enters the space fully, and touches her shoulder.*

HOPE

Oh Henry.

LUKE

You should run those fingers under some cold water. Come on sweety, Uncle Luke will take care of you.

HOPE

Luke?

LUKE

Come on, come here little one.

HOPE *and* LUKE *embrace and sway gently around the room.*

HOPE

Where did you go when you died Luke?

LUKE

Don't worry your pretty little head about that. You'll soon find out.

HOPE

Do you still love me?

LUKE

Shhhh now.

She breaks away.

HOPE

Did you ever love me?

LUKE

You were the brightest, shiniest thing in my life.

HOPE

I was eleven years old.

LUKE

What a long time I loved you.

He begins to fondle her breasts.

HOPE

You did me such wrong.

HOPE *pushes him away. The sound of keys, and voices at the door.*

HOPE

Do you know what I really wish?

LUKE *begins to retreat and finally fades from sight, as* HENRY *enters.*

HOPE

I wished that you'd loved someone more than me.

HENRY

Hope?

HOPE

Yeah yeah. I'm all right.

HENRY

Talking to yourself.

HOPE

Yeah. You know. Just sorting stuff out.

HENRY

Talking of stuff, there's/something I need to tell you.

HOPE

/Stuff about me god how boring you know stuff stuff stuff. Stuff about what a completely, ugly person I am.

HENRY

Darling can we talk about this later maybe?

The door burst open. KATIE *enters and walks up to* HOPE, *then goes to slap her across the face.* HENRY *restrains her.*

KATIE

How dare you. Both of you.

HENRY

Now Katie we talked about this in the lift.

KATIE

Get your hands off me you piece of filth.

HENRY

I'm sorry Hope. I had to tell her. She loves you too.

KATIE *and* HOPE *stare at each other.* HENRY *stays out of the way.*

HOPE

Katie, they're going to cut my breasts off. I'll never be able to feed my babies.

KATIE *embraces* HOPE.

KATIE

[*Rocking her*] There there honey. Katie's here now.

Scene 5

Sydney. A private hospital room, after the operation. The NURSE *sorts some flowers out then sits holding* HOPE*'s hand while she sleeps. An Australian bush ballad can be heard, but stops when* HOPE *awakes.*

HOPE

Say something nice to me.

NURSE

You're rich.

HOPE *laughs.*

HOPE

Yes, I am.

NURSE

You must have lots of friends too judging from these flowers. Most of them from overseas. You're not famous or anything are you? Maybe I should take some pictures of the new you and sell them to Kerry Packer's mob.

More laughter.

NURSE

And who's this Julian bloke? He sure sends a mean bunch.

HOPE

My ex.

NURSE

Ah. A few cards from Condobolin too. That's a long ways from London. Or Sydney for that matter.

HOPE

Not far enough.

NURSE

Know what you mean. I'm from West Wyalong.

HOPE

Want to run away to London with me? Know anything about banking?

NURSE

I think I've got about as much chance as you have of getting to London ... oh my god oh I am so sorry, god they usually put me in intensive care where everyone's out of it 'cause I've got such a big mouth.

HOPE

Don't worry.

NURSE

Sorry.

HOPE

But I need to be alone for a bit please.

NURSE

Seriously though Mrs Jackson, you ...

HOPE

Please call me Hope. God you make me feel like I'm 100. Now go away.

NURSE

Hope. It's time to take a look at yourself.

HOPE

I've been doing far too much of that all my life thank you very much.

NURSE

You've got physio this afternoon. And I have to change your bandages.

HOPE

I'm still a bit tired.

NURSE

The Doctor will be along soon and she won't be bullied.

HOPE

So.

NURSE

So.

Pause

HOPE

How long.

NURSE

I don't think we'll be able to keep our date for the next mardi-gras sweetheart.

NURSE *holds her hand.* HOPE *feigns sleep. Nurse makes sure she's comfortable then exits. The music returns.* HOPE *automates her bed to rise to a sitting position and witnesses her dead mother* DESTINY*'s arrival. The music fades.*

DESTINY

[*Singing*] 'I love you, you love me, that's how simple life can be' [*fades into a nervous hum as she makes herself comfortable on a chair, still sometimes snipping with the scissors*]. Ah. Hello love.

HOPE

Hello mother. Thanks for the genes.

DESTINY

Well I would have been suspicious of any other welcome, so you're not too out of sorts then.

HOPE

What do you want mother?

DESTINY

I've just come to say goodbye to my baby.

HOPE

Well goodbye and thank you very bloody much for everything.

DESTINY

It's OK to hate your mother Hope.

HOPE

I don't hate you. I just miss you. I always missed you.

During the following DESTINY *changes* HOPE*'s bandages, and later brushes / plaits her hair.* HOPE *slips back into childhood.*

DESTINY

Do you know sweetheart, you shouldn't blame yourself about Daddy. Remember what that useless priest said at his funeral, god do you remember his cowboy boots? And they said he drove the local tow truck in Deniliquin. Useful for giving last rites in the worst cases I suppose. But he said something during the service that just plain unlocked my grief and sent it flying. He said that more Vietnam vets had committed suicide since they'd been home than soldiers actually died in the war. Now you know your Daddy and me fought a lot, but what you probably can't remember is how much I loved him. But one day I turned around to find him gone, just vanished. I didn't vanish him. I just wasn't in his heart anymore. For ages I'd blamed that bloody tractor accident. Then all that stuff with Luke and me and bloody money. Plus me being such a slut surely didn't help. And after you left he was really lonely, and I looked at him one day and suddenly realised that I didn't know anything about him. But by then I was too bloody worn out to try. People shouldn't have to be on their own through all the hard things in life my beautiful little girl. Now you listen to me Hope. Darling, you've got to make room in your heart for love. Let all this pain go. Mummy's very very sorry that she didn't take proper care of you.

HOPE

Mummy, I don't like Uncle Luke.

DESTINY

I know sweetheart. I know. Everything will be alright.

Scene 6

Lunch at Sydney restaurant, some time after the operation.

COMPANION 1

Well she doesn't look that bad.

COMPANION 2

No.

COMPANION 3

Are you sure they cut them off?

COMPANION 2

Don't be a dickhead, they're falsies. For God's sake.

COMPANION 1

Stop staring at them you bloody idiot.

COMPANION 3

Sorry. Sorry. Shit, it's just that. Well. You know.

COMPANION 2

Oh who doesn't bloody know for christsakes. You're probably one of the reasons she left the country in the first place.

COMPANION 1

Yeah. Imagine having to wake up next to your ugly face.

COMPANION 3

Give us a break. Anyway. We're wasting our time, sshh here she comes, she won't say yes.

HOPE *enters.*

COMPANION 1

What makes you so sure?

HOPE

Sure about what?

COMPANION 3

Oh. You know. This and that.

HOPE

What?

COMPANION 2

Whether or not you love us. Whether or not you'd rather run your farm and retreat to hicksville. Whether or not we'll win the cricket. Whether or not our lovely Prime Minister will ever say sorry.

COMPANION 3

To the bloody whinging abos. Yeah. Like that's a good idea.

COMPANION 1 & 2

Shut up you dickhead!

COMPANION 1

Sorry about him Hope. He's a bit . . .

COMPANION 3

What! What am I?! Jesus.

COMPANION 1

Drunk.

COMPANION 2

Racist.

COMPANION 3

Hey! I'm paying for this bloody lunch. Me. Herr Director. And it doesn't matter what you think I am Hope the fact of the matter is and we all know it that we're the best in the country, in South East Asia to be more precise, and if you don't want to come on board with us you can just piss off back to England. I'm sure you know the way.

HOPE

Would you go to war?

COMPANION 3

What?

HOPE

Would you? Go off to war and kill for something you believed would make the world a better place.

COMPANION 3

Jesus.

During the following HOPE*'s dead father enters and observes.*

HOPE

My dad could never eat eggs again after Vietnam. He said they came in tins or something over there.

COMPANION 2

Fuck Vietnam. We'll make you an equal partner Hope.

HOPE

So many stolen things.

COMPANION 1

Your remission could be long enough to make us all rich Hope. You can buy a lot of things back with the serious kind of money we're talking about.

HOPE

Look. Thanks very much for your offer. But no.

HOPE *rises.*

HOPE

See yas round like a rissole.

HOPE *exits with her father.*

COMPANION 3

She always was a bloody loony.

COMPANION 2

You really are a complete dickhead Barry, you do know that?

Scene 7

HOPE *and* HENRY *and* KATIE *are in a car in crowded city traffic. Nobody is talking.* HOPE *is smoking. The cricket is on the radio. Australia is losing. At the next traffic lights/stop in the flow of traffic* HOPE *leans forward from the back seat and kisses them both, then gets out of the car.*

KATIE

There goes your life long fantasy Henry.

HENRY *jumps out the car.*

HENRY

Hope. Come back.

KATIE

Let her go Henry. Let her go.

HENRY *returns.* KATIE *comforts him.*

KATIE

Looks like it's just you and me and the endless bloody paddocks.

HENRY *slumps over the wheel, not even revived by the victorious shouts of 'Howzat' from the radio.*

Scene 8

Before. HOPE *is ironing in her beachside Sydney apartment, ridiculous things like underwear. Sound of the surf can be heard above the talk-back-radio station.*

RADIO ANNOUNCER

Surely you don't think that's true?

GUEST

Well yes I do. I think we should all vote no. Otherwise we'll have the politicians running the country good and proper for ever. Now I'm as Australian as the next person but if you vote yes to becoming a republic/

RADIO ANNOUNCER

/I certainly will be.

GUEST

Well if you vote yes then we're all doomed.

RADIO ANNOUNCER

That's a bit melodramatic surely?

GUEST

No way. Look. Of course I want us to become a republic. But not under these conditions, conditions that mean if we vote yes we're going to let the Prime Minister and his mates choose the President. That choice should be a decision for the people. We have to cut our ties to the past properly, with dignity.

HENRY *knocks and enters.*

RADIO ANNOUNCER

Well the people will be making their decision soon enough. Thanks to our guests on today's program for

HENRY *turns the radio off.*

HENRY

All packed then?

HOPE

What?

HENRY

All packed I said.

HENRY *unplugs the iron.*

HENRY

Hope?

HOPE

Yeah.

HENRY

You've made up your mind then? About moving back to the farm with me.

HOPE

Not you Henry. You and Katie.

HENRY

Us then. After the . . . after . . .

HOPE

Operation. The operation.

Silence

HENRY

Katie reckons you should tell the surgeons to cut out all the other shit inside you while they're in there.

HOPE

[*Laughs*] Yeah. Why not. [*Pause*] Thanks Henry. Going home sounds real good. [*Hugging herself*] Fancy a last squeeze?

Scene 9

Now. HOPE *is at a crowded Sydney beach on a hot summer day. Noises of thunderous surf, birds, angry parents and children. A set of crossed flags as well as a 'beach closed' sign indicate the dangerous conditions. The lighting changes dramatically as* HOPE *rises from her towel, sensing the afternoon storm.*

HOPE

Everyone is leaving.

HOPE *builds a sandcastle.*

HOPE

I reckon that more people kill themselves in the bush because they can't see where anything ends. I like that about Sydney. Its edges.

HOPE *enters the water.*

HOPE

I love the beach in a storm. And there'll be a king tide tonight.

BEACH INSPECTOR

[*Off, through a megaphone*] You. There. Please come out of the water.

HOPE *goes deeper.*

HOPE

My mother said that I came out of her womb swimming. First one arm shot out, then the other, and then the rest of me. I dove into the world.

HOPE *dives beneath the waves.*

BEACH INSPECTOR

[*Off, through a megaphone*] Come out of the surf now. The Beach is closed. You. There. In the pink swimmers. GET OUT OF THE WATER NOW.

HOPE

It was a really smooth entry.

HOPE *removes her false breasts and throws them in the direction of the beach inspector.*

BEACH INSPECTOR

[*Off, through a megaphone*] This is your last warning, lady. There is a dangerous rip out there. GET OUT OF THE WATER NOW. [*Aside*] Christ get the duck out boys looks like we've got a psycho on our hands. We'll have to go get the stupid bitch.

HOPE *floats. The storm breaks. Behind a scrim the storm continues and the clubbies prepare the rubber dinghy for their futile rescue operation.* HOPE *is nowhere to be found. She leaves the water.*

HOPE

Lady. Ladyladyladyladyladyladylady. So many smooth entries in a lady, so easy to find and use. Lady lady lady the beach is closed you bloody fucking moron I KNOW THAT.

HOPE *wraps herself in one of the beach flags after removing it. She watches the clubbies abandon the rescue attempt. A silent light from an emergency vehicle flashes. Dusk.*

HOPE

'Bloody stupid bitch'. I could hear them cursing me through my thick drowning. 'Bloody stupid bitch'. On and on and on, as if they had nothing to do with it. Nothing at all.

Silence

HOPE

We're quitters, us Jacksons. Pathetic mob that we are. Squatters worn out by a squalid history. I think, next time round, I'll stay home and fight. I'll make the whole damn world say sorry.

HOPE *returns to the ocean. Night falls. The tide comes in. The moon rises.*

THE END

Providence

Characters

LIBERTY, *the wife, twenty something*
DAN, *the husband, thirty something*
BRONTE, *the best friend, slightly older*

Set

The edge of a lake; DAN *and* LIBERTY*'s home.*

Scene 1

The lake, a late winter afternoon.

DAN *and* LIBERTY *are entwined and rolling around, laughing, on a rug by the edge of a lake.* BRONTE *is lying in a hammock.* LIBERTY *jumps up, grabs her camera, and takes a photo of* DAN, *then walks over to* BRONTE *and does the same.*

BRONTE

Go away. I'm sleeping.

LIBERTY

You look beautiful, just floating there in the sun.

BRONTE

You do.

LIBERTY

It'll be a great photo.

BRONTE

Sure. The way I feel.

LIBERTY

You'll feel better soon.

BRONTE

Yeah. If I get any sleep.

LIBERTY

Just checking.

BRONTE

Thanks. I love you too, now piss off.

LIBERTY *kisses her on the forehead and returns to* DAN, *who has been skipping stones on the lake.*

DAN

She'll get over it—he was a deadshit.

LIBERTY

True.

DAN

[*Pause*] So?

LIBERTY

So?

DAN

Will you?

LIBERTY

No!

DAN

Why not?

LIBERTY

Because you resent my money, and my family, and you're a pig.

DAN

I am not!

LIBERTY

You're a pig for women.

DAN

Not any more Liberty.

LIBERTY

And your poetry, and your research, and your teaching. And your endless bloody mates. And football, and surfing, and . . .

DAN

And you–you first.

LIBERTY

I'm not going to help your writing–unless you think about poetry while you're fucking.

DAN

What's wrong with that?

LIBERTY

So long as the poem is about me . . .

DAN

All my poems are about you.

LIBERTY

Liar.

DAN

Marry me.

LIBERTY

No, I said!

DAN

Liberty. Please.

LIBERTY

Only if you swim across the lake. And back.

DAN

If that's what you want [*he partially undresses*].

LIBERTY

No! It's freezing. Come here. If I marry you I have to believe you love me more than anything. Anything.

DAN

Do you love me? Do you?

LIBERTY

God you really are paranoid.

DAN

No. [*Pause*] I'm just a cautious, newly appointed modern poetry lecturer. Down on his knees, begging.

LIBERTY

What! Dan! You got the job!

DAN

The pay's lousy of course. But I'm sure to get ahead eventually—if I keep churning out the poems and I don't root any more of my adoring, young, nubile students.

LIBERTY

I'm so happy for you. Wow. God. Bronte'll be glad to have you in the Department. After all those old fogeys. Oh Dan, I am so excited for you.

DAN

It's a long way from the abattoirs, that's for sure.

LIBERTY

I'd still love you if you were a butcher.

DAN

I bet.

LIBERTY

You must've known you'd never end up there, though, surely?

DAN

Maybe. Bronte always said we'd go to uni and be 'real smart'. 'Bronte Brown Owl', my mum used to call her, ringleader extraordinaire.

LIBERTY

I can imagine. Commandant of the local kids gang.

DAN

You're not wrong. I remember I used to tell everyone she was my sister.

So they'd like me more.

LIBERTY

She might as well be.

DAN

Yeah.

LIBERTY

Funny how you both ended up in the same place.

DAN

Spooky.

LIBERTY

You're so close. I thought you were, you know, 'together' when I first met you. I can imagine why her husband was so jealous, actually.

DAN

Lots of people thought we were a couple. It was a defence tactic I suppose, sticking together all through uni. We were both so intimidated by everyone. [*Pause*] We were the only students we knew who didn't jet off overseas every summer holidays.

LIBERTY

Are you having a go at me?

DAN

Yes. Now marry me before I change my mind.

LIBERTY

Fuck you.

DAN

Go on then.

LIBERTY

I love you. I can't sleep alone since I met you.

DAN

You won't have to. I promise.

They lie back on the rug.

BRONTE

If I hadn't been so comfortable in this hammock, this protective web, then things might have turned out differently. But I was so at peace here on the edge of this giant lake that I never wanted to leave. I was intoxicated by Dan, and Libby, and the grey, constant sunshine of the late afternoon. Accepting bliss. But it's when you relax that things usually go wrong. I wasn't very prudent. Hardly a manifestation of divine care.

BRONTE *leaves the hammock and walks towards* DAN *and* LIBERTY, *who are now sitting silently waiting for the sunset. They occasionally kiss.*

BRONTE

Look at them. Watch them kissing. When she lays her head on his green jumper, her hair turns gently green, and soon the colour travels down her whole body. And when she kisses him, with those red lips, full of blood not yet squeezed out from too much talking, then he turns very slowly but hotly red. So that soon, when they kiss, they are the same colour. But for how long?

BRONTE *joins* LIBERTY *and* DAN, *just as* LIBERTY *whispers something in* DAN*'s ear.*

DAN

Yes Yes Yes!

BRONTE

Told her the good news then?

DAN

Yes / but that's not it.

LIBERTY

/ Dan!

BRONTE

What?

DAN

She's caved in!

LIBERTY

I said we should wait, Dan. Before blurting it out to the world.

BRONTE

Don't tell me?

DAN

Yes!

BRONTE

I don't believe it.

BRONTE *sits down on the rug between them.*

LIBERTY

Sorry, Bronte. It's a bit insensitive, considering.

BRONTE

Don't be silly!

DAN

She's alright Libby. Eh Bronte? Be happy for us?

BRONTE

Congratulations. What took you so long?

LIBERTY

He's so old fashioned he had to have a job first.

DAN

Yeah, right.

LIBERTY

What then?

DAN

Just, you know, sorting out my shit.

BRONTE

Finished already?

DAN

Piss off.

LIBERTY

Don't start you two.

DAN

Tell her to stop.

BRONTE

What? Being smarter than you?

DAN

Slag.

LIBERTY

Quit it! You're both mad to want to be academics anyway. I can't wait to get out of uni and into the real world.

DAN

What's that supposed to mean?

LIBERTY

Touchy!

DAN

Anyway, you won't be going anywhere for now.

LIBERTY

What do you mean?

BRONTE

She can't stay here editing the *Student News* forever Dan.

DAN

There's plenty of other jobs around. No need to leave town.

LIBERTY

And there's plenty of papers in that big, nasty city you crawled out of, one of which has already offered me a job. Remember?

DAN

You're not seriously considering it are you?

LIBERTY

I didn't promise to be a faculty wife, Dan. That's not why I did a Masters in journalism.

DAN

Suit yourself.

BRONTE

In a generous mood are we then?

LIBERTY

I have to work you know.

DAN

Not there you don't.

BRONTE

It's not too far to drive.

DAN

Hours every day!

BRONTE

Worth it though—it's a lucky break.

LIBERTY

Exactly.

DAN

It's a trashy metropolitan tabloid.

LIBERTY

Dan!

BRONTE

Now, now, that's enough.

LIBERTY

I reckon.

DAN

I'm sorry.

LIBERTY

So you should be.

DAN

I am. Really. I just want to spend as much time as possible with you.

LIBERTY

On your terms!

BRONTE

She's right.

DAN

I said I'm sorry.

LIBERTY

Anyway. I haven't decided yet.

DAN

You know best. Sweetheart. Darling.

LIBERTY

Stop crawling and do something useful, like make a fire. I'll go up to the house and get something to drink. Red? To match the sunset?

DAN

Yeah. Lot's of it.

Liberty leaves.

BRONTE

I'll just race up and get some fags.

She chases LIBERTY. DAN *starts collecting stones and lays them in a circle, then some driftwood. He makes a fire while the women talk out of his hearing.*

LIBERTY

I'll be right. Keep Dan company.

BRONTE

I wanted to apologise for being narky. It just took me by surprise.

LIBERTY

Don't apologise, I'm sorry. Shit, we came up here to celebrate your divorce.

BRONTE

Forget it. Liberty—do you know what you're letting yourself in for?

LIBERTY

I think so.

BRONTE

I don't mean marriage. I mean Dan.

LIBERTY

I know what he's like Bronte.

BRONTE

I've seen him bugger up tougher women than you.

LIBERTY

[*Pause*] I know I can help him.

BRONTE

Ah.

LIBERTY

His childhood is long gone. No one can hurt him any more. I'm just going to teach him that.

BRONTE

Do you think he'll believe you?

LIBERTY

Look. Thanks for caring. But I'm more worried about you to be honest.

BRONTE

No need. [*Pause*] Shit it's freezing out here now.

LIBERTY

Go and let Dan warm you up. I'll be back soon.

LIBERTY *leaves.* BRONTE *returns to the fire.*

DAN

Gotta light? [*He finds his own and lights the fire*] You OK?

BRONTE

Yeah. You?

DAN

Yeah.

BRONTE

Bit shocked.

DAN

Me too. I still can't believe she loves me.

BRONTE

Yeah, you're such an arsehole.

DAN

You love it.

BRONTE

Seriously, why shouldn't she?

DAN

Because I'm a wolf. Because we're from completely different worlds.

BRONTE

Your worlds aren't so different now.

DAN

Come and sit next to me. [*She does*] We're the same, you and me. We'll always reek faintly of trash.

BRONTE

Fuck you.

DAN

But it's different with Liberty. I need someone the opposite of myself.

BRONTE

Good luck. It didn't work for me.

DAN

Don't jinx me.

BRONTE

Goodness made me soft. I got so soft I couldn't think any more.

DAN

He wasn't too bad to you, was he?

BRONTE

No! I was bad to him. He blamed himself for my unhappiness, so he just got nicer and nicer till I vomited. I was the cruel one.

DAN

Maybe you should have married someone like me.

BRONTE

[*Sings*] 'I fell in/to a burning ring of fire.'

DAN

Yeah, yeah.

BRONTE

[*Sings*] 'I went down, down, down . . . '

DAN

Shut up.

BRONTE

[*Sings*] 'And the flames, they got higher . . . '

DAN

Just shut up, will you? No more fire dancing.

BRONTE

Here, here.

DAN

I mean it. Libby'll fix everything.

BRONTE

Yes. She's good at that. [*Pause*] God. Sometimes I wish I'd never introduced you.

DAN

Give us a break. [*Silence*] I'll say it for you. [*Pause*] 'Be good to her Dan. Don't ever / hurt her.'

BRONTE

/ If you ever did, I'd . . . I'd hate you.

DAN

That'd make two of us.

BRONTE

These last six months Liberty's been the best friend to me. All through that last ugly bowel movement of my marriage. The best you could ever want.

DAN

I know what you mean. That's how she makes me feel too.

BRONTE

Promise to be good. Dan?

DAN

Promise.

BRONTE

I don't know if I can trust you.

DAN

What do you mean? I promised, what more do you want me to do, cut off my hands?

BRONTE

Prove it to me. That I can trust you. Tell me, if I sat on top of you right now, and kissed you, and asked you to fuck me, what would you do?

He doesn't answer. She sits on top of him.

BRONTE

What would you do? [*She kisses him*] Would you come with me over there, where it's dark, and make love to me? You would, wouldn't you?

Suddenly DAN *over turns* BRONTE, *pinning her down.*

DAN

What would you do?

BRONTE

Go right ahead. I'm not married any more.

DAN

I am.

BRONTE

Almost.

He releases her.

DAN

You're a bitch.

BRONTE

It's nothing personal. Against Liberty. I was only testing.

DAN

Crap.

BRONTE

Crap yourself. You don't believe in monogamy any more than I do.

DAN

I believe in Liberty.

BRONTE

Sure you do.

DAN

You don't believe in anyone.

BRONTE

Maybe. Look at it this way. It's like if you ever hit Libby, I'd automatically be on her side—nothing against you personally. So don't test me about it. I hate taking sides.

DAN

You do want me don't you?

BRONTE

[*Pause*] In theory. [*Pause*] Why couldn't you have married someone I could hate and make my life easier?

DAN

Why didn't you sit on top of me years ago?

BRONTE

Too many girls around. You were too precious. I thought you'd reject me. I was right.

DAN

Wrong. But it just aint gonna happen in this life.

BRONTE

I guess I'll take what I can. It's what I'm used to.

DAN

Don't be hurt.

BRONTE

Because you want her? No. But I would be if you ever hurt her. Make it worthwhile for once Dan.

LIBERTY *returns carrying a parcel and some wine.*

BRONTE

I'll be watching you.

DAN

Thank you.

LIBERTY

Hey, look what I've got.

She throws the parcel at DAN *and opens the wine.*

LIBERTY

It came in the post. If that's what I think it is, we're in for a big celebration. Is it?

DAN

[*Opening parcel*] You're not wrong. Fuck me. What a beautiful sight.

BRONTE

Give us a look [*she grabs a book*].

He kisses one of his books and throws it straight into the fire.

DAN

I sacrifice my first born in the hope that all my devils leave me.

LIBERTY

Well. That was melodramatic.

BRONTE

Plenty more where they came from.

DAN

To us three. A toast to love, to poetry. [*They toast*] And to success.

LIBERTY

Success!

BRONTE

Success!

LIBERTY

I'm so proud of you.

BRONTE

Hey, take a look at the dedication.

LIBERTY

[*Does so*] Dan!

BRONTE

Bit soppy.

DAN

I mean it. Thanks Liberty [*they kiss.*].

BRONTE

Congratulations, Dan. I am extremely jealous. And on that note, I think I might leave.

LIBERTY

How come? Don't be silly.

DAN

Hell no!

BRONTE

I've already stayed too long. And you two need some time alone. I do too.

LIBERTY

Please don't Bronte.

DAN

Yeah, stay.

BRONTE

No.

LIBERTY

Please?

DAN

Remember our first time here together? We got pissed and tried to swim to Canada.

LIBERTY

And we saw all those flying fish by the moonlight.

BRONTE

It feels so long ago.

DAN

Stay.

BRONTE

It's too cold.

DAN

Share my blanket with me, girls. Oh come on, I deserve a party.

BRONTE

OK [*they sit*].

DAN

The Trinity reunited.

BRONTE

For the the last time?

DAN

Never!

LIBERTY

[*Pause, she looks across the lake*] Do you ever wish you could fly?

BRONTE *stands up and walks around the fire while* DAN *and* LIBERTY *freeze.*

BRONTE

I'm glad I stayed, because that was one of the last great times we had together. I tried so hard, but their marriage pushed us further away from each other, and life wore us down a little too much. We were all of us made of sandstone, eroding more with each high tide. Regardless, I continued my vigilance—love binds you. But . . .

She stops and stares at them. Their arms are around each other.

BRONTE

. . . for the moment, we're still here. Our arms sit lightly around each other with such tenderness that it's erotic. We don't need to speak. We just sit real close to each other and dream of flying, laughing little soundless bubbles of joy, and softly share some cigarettes with the lake.

LIBERTY *and* DAN *break their freeze.*

DAN

Come here.

He lights cigarettes for all them. BRONTE *once again sits in the middle. She turns and kisses* DAN *first, then* LIBERTY. DAN *and* LIBERTY *lean towards each other behind* BRONTE*'s back and kiss. Then they all lie back together on the rug and look at the stars.*

Scene 2

DAN and LIBERTY's home, three years later, early evening. LIBERTY and DAN are eating dinner. The setting and atmosphere is romantic, but they eat in silence. The phone rings.

DAN

Let the answering machine get it.

LIBERTY

No, I can't.

DAN

Leave it, Liberty.

LIBERTY

Dan I / shouldn't, considering . . .

DAN

/ Please. We haven't had a meal together in weeks. Why are you so fucking obsessed with work lately?

LIBERTY

I am not.

ANSWERING MACHINE

[DAN*'s voice*] Hi. This is the Fitzgerald-Baker residence. You know the routine. / Talk to you soon.

LIBERTY

/ See?

ANSWERING MACHINE

[*Man's voice*] Pick up the phone Libby. It's me [*they continue eating*]. Liberty? Ah, um—well . . . Liberty? Are you there? Shit. Maybe you've heard the news and you're at Dylan's. So, um, I'll try there. If not, ring me as soon as you're back. OK. Bye.

LIBERTY

I wonder what's up?

DAN

Your boss freaks out about everything.

LIBERTY

True.

DAN

Why would he think you'd be at Dylan's?

LIBERTY

We're covering the story together. Public can't get enough press when it comes to serial killers. Just this afternoon the police discovered . . . [*She realises* DAN *is not listening*]. Am I boring you?

DAN

What?

LIBERTY

[*Pause*] So how's work for you?

DAN

Let's talk about something else.

LIBERTY

OK. How do you like the wine? Dylan brought it back from Adelaide.

DAN

It's not bad. Actually, it's shit. But, hey, a hangover is a hangover!

LIBERTY

Planning a big night, are we?

DAN

I wouldn't mind.

LIBERTY

How is work then?

DAN

Fine.

LIBERTY

Really?

DAN *stops eating and starts pacing around, drinking more.*

DAN

Fucked, really. I don't think the Department is going to renew my contract. I'll find out tomorrow.

LIBERTY

Why on earth not? Surely your latest book / will impress everyone.

DAN

/ It's a piddling little book of poems with a minuscule print run that'll still be on the shelf in 2096.

LIBERTY

Oh Dan don't be so negative. It's a powerful collection. [*Pause*] A bit brutal, but / undoubtedly powerful . . .

DAN

/ What do you mean?

LIBERTY

I didn't mean anything, it's a powerful collection, like I said.

DAN

No. Tell me what you mean.

LIBERTY

You're so sensitive.

DAN

Brutal and sensitive? Make up your mind.

LIBERTY

You used to write love poems Dan.

DAN

What's it matter anyway? No one is interested in poetry any more.

LIBERTY

I'm sorry you're on tenderhooks about your job again.

DAN

[*Silence*] This is the longest conversation I've had with you for a month. Do you realise that?

LIBERTY

Yes.

DAN

What's the matter with you?

LIBERTY

This is a big break for me, Dan, you know that's why I've been working so much overtime. I've been hitting the front page so often it makes Reuters look like they've got writers block! I thought you'd be pleased for me.

DAN

I'm so pleased for you my food just sticks in my throat. I'm all choked up.

LIBERTY

Don't start Dan. Shit, you wonder why I don't talk to you!

The phone rings. DAN *grabs it.*

DAN

Hello. Yes. Hang on. It's for you, ace.

LIBERTY

Yes. Hi. [*Long pause while* DAN *paces menacingly*] I see. OK. I'll be right there. [*She hangs up*] Look. I'm sorry about your job, but you hate teaching anyway. Just tell the uni to go jump. We can live off my money, you can write in peace at home. We'll be all right. Things always work out for us.

DAN

Do they?

LIBERTY

I'm sorry, Dan, but I have to go.

DAN

So I gather.

LIBERTY

They've found another body.

DAN

I completely understand.

LIBERTY

I really have to go. [*Gathering some things together, nervously*] Can you believe it, they think the killer is a woman! It turns out that all the victims / had at one time been charged with rape but got . . .

DAN *stands and moves quickly around to* LIBERTY, *catching her off guard. He pushes* LIBERTY *hard and slams her into the wall, pinning her there.*

LIBERTY

Dan, please don't, not now. Calm down, let's both calm down.

He pushes her again, provokingly.

DAN

Come on.

LIBERTY

Let me go. You'll only regret it.

DAN

Tell me where you're really going.

LIBERTY

I don't want to fight Dan. Not now.

DAN

You think you can just ignore me?

He pushes her roughly again, trying to get her to fight back.

DAN

When I need you so much?

LIBERTY

Please Dan, stop it. I'm going to go whether you hit me or not.

He punches her in the face and she falls to the ground. LIBERTY *slowly gets up, and straightens herself.*

DAN

Why do you do this to me?

LIBERTY

[*Long pause*] I have to go. We'll talk about this when I come home.

DAN

Or will you run around to Dylan's for some sympathy?

LIBERTY *slaps his face. He slaps her back.* DAN *paces, frantic.*

LIBERTY

It doesn't make any difference what I do, does it? Not any more.

LIBERTY *holds her face, in pain, while she gathers her things.*

LIBERTY

You shouldn't drink when you feel like this.

DAN

Shouldn't I? What should I do?

He is threatening, and closing in on LIBERTY *again.*

DAN

It makes me feel a lot better you know. A lot fucking better than you do.

He pushes her against the wall again, and she drops all her things to shield herself. He breaks out of his anger and is suddenly frightened. DAN *looks at* LIBERTY *and realises what he's done, and collapses at the table.*

DAN

I'm sorry. I'm so sorry.

LIBERTY *starts collecting her things, thinks better of it, and comes over to comfort him. As she puts her arm on him he recoils, and goes and sits in the corner on the floor.*

LIBERTY

Don't freak me out more than I am already Dan. Get up. Look at yourself.

DAN

I can't.

LIBERTY

Look at me then. You're going to have to look me in the eye some time.

LIBERTY *dips a table napkin in her wine glass and wipes the blood off her face. She sits down on the floor a safe distance away from* DAN.

LIBERTY

Jesus, Dan, what did I do to deserve that? What did I do this time?

DAN

I don't know. I can't control myself.

LIBERTY

You've really hurt me.

DAN

I'm sorry.

LIBERTY

People are going to notice this. What am I supposed to say?

DAN

Please don't leave me.

DAN *crawls over to* LIBERTY.

LIBERTY

Why do you hate me?

DAN

I don't. I don't.

LIBERTY

Yes you do. Just before you hit me, you hate me.

DAN

I . . . get . . . so . . . frightened.

LIBERTY

You do? That's rich.

DAN

Please Libby, forgive me.

LIBERTY

You make it so hard Dan.

DAN

I love you. If you give up on me I don't know if I could go on.

He crawls up into her arms, she rocks him soothingly.

LIBERTY

Everything will be all right. Trust me.

DAN

Help me, Libby.

LIBERTY

I'm doing the best I can.

DAN

I love you.

LIBERTY

Yes.

He starts to kiss her.

LIBERTY

Don't. Not now. Come on. Let me go Dan.

DAN

I'll never let you go.

Their kissing continues. LIBERTY *resists only at first.* DAN *stops after a while and stares at her. He strokes her face where he had struck her.*

LIBERTY

Is this all we're ever going to have?

DAN

Is that up to me?

LIBERTY *starts kissing* DAN, *who responds. The phone rings. They ignore it and continue. Blackout as the answering machine switches on.*

ANSWERING MACHINE

Hi. This is the Fitzgerald-Baker residence. You know the routine.

Scene 3

DAN *and* LIBERTY*'s home, the next morning.*

DAN

Libby. Liberty Unlock the door. Come on. Please. I have to leave for work.

He shakes the bathroom door violently.

DAN

Liberty. Let me in. I won't hurt you.

LIBERTY*'s crying can be heard from behind the closed door.*

DAN

Liberty, please open the door.

LIBERTY

Leave me alone. Just go away.

DAN

I have to get to work Liberty. Please. Let me talk to you.

LIBERTY

No.

DAN

Listen. I've phoned Bronte. She's coming over.

LIBERTY

What? What did you tell her?

DAN

Nothing. I just told her to come.

LIBERTY

I don't want her to see me like this.

DAN

Let me help you Liberty. Please, I'm sorry.

LIBERTY

You were sorry last night too.

The doorbell rings.

LIBERTY

Don't let her in.

DAN

I can't leave you alone Libby, not like this. If you don't let me in I'll be / sick with worry all day.

LIBERTY

/ Why should I? You'll just cry and need comfort and I've got no energy left for anyone anymore not even me so just fuck off!

DAN *collapses outside the door. The doorbell rings again and again. He drags himself up to let* BRONTE *in.*

BRONTE

Morning. What's all this about?

DAN

Hi Bronte. I . . . I have to go.

BRONTE

Where's Liberty?

DAN

She's locked herself in the bathroom. I can't talk any sense into her, and I can't stay, I have a meeting with the Dean.

BRONTE

What happened?

BRONTE *goes over to the bathroom door and knocks.*

BRONTE

Liberty? It's me. What's going on? What's wrong?

She hears LIBERTY *running the bath.*

BRONTE

Will somebody tell me why you dragged me out of bed and all the way over here? Frankly I've got better things / to do.

DAN

/ I hit her.

BRONTE

You what?

DAN

I hit her.

BRONTE *goes back and bangs on the bathroom door.*

BRONTE

Liberty open the door right now and let me in.

DAN

I . . .

BRONTE

What happened?

DAN

We had a bad fight. I hit her. Last night. And then she started at me again this morning and I started at her and now she's in there and won't talk to me.

BRONTE

How bad?

DAN

It was bad, all right? I've been bad. I beat my own wife, who loves me. Don't you understand how that makes me feel?

BRONTE

I think you should go.

DAN

Yes. Tell her . . .

BRONTE

Now would be a good time.

DAN *goes to leave and* BRONTE *grabs him.*

BRONTE

How could you do this?

DAN

I don't know.

BRONTE

How long has it been going on?

DAN

For a while. Since you stopped watching me, I guess.

BRONTE

Ah. It's my fault?

DAN

You told me / you'd watch me.

BRONTE

/ I told you not to make me take sides. [*Pause*] What's happened to you?

DAN

What's happened to all of us?

BRONTE *watches as* DAN *leaves then goes to the bathroom door.*

BRONTE

He's gone Libby. Let me in.

LIBERTY

I'm in the bath. I've unlocked the door.

BRONTE

Can I come in then?

LIBERTY

I suppose so.

BRONTE *opens the bathroom door and stands there.*

BRONTE

You OK?

LIBERTY

Yeah.

BRONTE

What happened?

LIBERTY

You heard. He hit me.

BRONTE

I can see that. Want a cup of tea or something?

LIBERTY

I wouldn't mind a drink to be honest. I've been at work most of the night. Haven't had any sleep.

BRONTE *mixes* LIBERTY *a drink.*

BRONTE

How come you had to work?

LIBERTY

Another murder.

BRONTE

So?

LIBERTY

I'm covering the story Bronte. Read the newspapers do you?

BRONTE

Oh. Right. Sorry.

LIBERTY *enters fresh from the bath.*

LIBERTY

Sure. Where's that drink?

BRONTE

Here it is, here. [*She turns to face* LIBERTY] Shit. I hate that man. How could he do that to you?

LIBERTY

I'm up for a promotion, you know.

BRONTE

He's hit you before, hasn't he?

LIBERTY

That would impress you both, wouldn't it? Little Liberty lurching to the top.

BRONTE

Hasn't he?

LIBERTY

Yes. He has.

BRONTE

I think you should go to the police Liberty.

LIBERTY

You have no idea, do you?

BRONTE

This is a mean thing to keep from me.

LIBERTY

I thought I could handle him. He's never been this bad before.

BRONTE

There's no excuse for it. Or for putting up with it.

LIBERTY

If you've come here to lecture me you can just leave right now.

BRONTE

You have to leave him. He won't stop now.

LIBERTY

I'm not going anywhere. You know very well that we have a passionate relationship Bronte, things'll work out.

BRONTE

What kind of shit is that? I can't believe I'm hearing you say this. Have you taken a look in the mirror?

LIBERTY

We've always had atrocious fights. And sometimes—sometimes—it gets physical. I hit him too you know.

BRONTE

So what?

LIBERTY

So what! So I'm just as fucked as he is OK?

BRONTE

No. He's twice as fucked. He's twice as big.

LIBERTY

When he's frightened he hits out. I shouldn't frighten him.

BRONTE

Can you hear yourself?

LIBERTY

You know very well what happened to him.

BRONTE

Is that how you justify it?

LIBERTY

No. It's how I forgive him.

BRONTE

[*Pause*] Let me take you to a doctor, at least.

LIBERTY

I should go. My head hurts.

BRONTE

I'm not surprised.

LIBERTY

I'll get dressed.

LIBERTY *goes off.*

BRONTE

The prick. The utter prick.

LIBERTY

You thought he was good enough for me when we got married.

BRONTE

Hmph.

LIBERTY

Maybe you should just stay out of this Bronte?

BRONTE

Hey. You phoned me.

LIBERTY

No. I didn't.

BRONTE *storms up to the door of* LIBERTY*'s bedroom where she is dressing.*

BRONTE

That's it. Fuck you. I will not, I refuse to, stand by and watch you get beaten up by your own husband. Leave him. You're too good for this. He's hurt you, don't you realise that? He beats you up for God's sake,

Liberty! What difference does it make why?

LIBERTY

[*She comes out of the room*] I'm pregnant.

BRONTE *stands there stunned.* LIBERTY *gives her a cuddle.*

BRONTE

Great. I hope it's a girl so she can keep up your tradition of dimwittedness.

LIBERTY

Hey. It's going to be all right. You're going to take me to the doctor. I'm going to say I fell over in the bath overcome by a surge of morning sickness. And you're going to sit there and wait for me.

BRONTE

You might be able to forgive him, Liberty, but how do you expect me to?

LIBERTY

He phoned you, didn't he? I didn't ask him to. And—he promised this morning he was going to get help.

BRONTE

Do you think he will?

LIBERTY

It's not like it's the first time he's promised. But I think this time he will.

BRONTE

Why?

LIBERTY

He just will, that's all.

BRONTE

How long? Just how long do you imagine you'll put up with it? Another five years? Seven? Nine? Leave him.

LIBERTY

I can't.

BRONTE

What do you mean, 'You can't'? How can you even contemplate subjecting a child to all this? Bloody hell, if I can turn my back on him after twenty something years / you certainly can.

LIBERTY

/ Could you? Honestly? Never see him again? Do you think I haven't tried before? Do you really think you could walk right out of here now and never see your best friend again? Just because of this?

BRONTE

I—I'd have to. I can make myself.

LIBERTY

What for? To punish him? Trust me. You'll be the loser.

BRONTE

I could live with it.

LIBERTY

Well I can't. You have no idea how much I love him.

BRONTE

Yes, I do. But I don't think he's worth it.

LIBERTY

I once believed that you would let me slice your ear off if it meant that you could have Dan instead of me.

BRONTE

Is that so? [*Pause*] Don't start fighting with me Liberty. I'm not the one who hurt you.

LIBERTY

Really? You've always made me feel like I'm not good enough for him.

BRONTE

Look, you're understandably upset . . .

LIBERTY

Answer me! You don't think I deserve him!

BRONTE

Deserve him! No. You don't. [*Pause*] Why on earth I let him marry you is beyond me. You were too innocent.

LIBERTY

Let him! Great. My husband is a wife basher and my girlfriend is a condescending bitch. And you can fuck right off with that 'innocence' crap.

BRONTE

You were. You were so much nicer than him. You were a nice girl from a nice place, who made us all feel very nice.

LIBERTY

Nice! Do you think my childhood was nicer than yours just because I was rich, just because there was a swimming pool in my back yard? Let me tell you something Bronte. In every swimming pool in the world there is an uncle beneath the surface, lurking there in his speedos, waiting for you, waiting to stick it right up you. Very politely, of course.

BRONTE

I see. So much for sharing everything with your best friend.

LIBERTY

Dan's my best friend. Not you. And it was hard enough telling him.

BRONTE

Dan the saviour.

LIBERTY

That's right.

BRONTE

Well, it's time to sack him. Why put up with any more shit?

LIBERTY

Believe me. I can tell a good man when I feel one. Even if it is through his fist.

BRONTE

You're gone. You are absolutely gone. He's fucked you right up.

LIBERTY

That's it, isn't it? That's your problem with all this. That he's fucked me, that all these years he's been fucking me and not you.

BRONTE

Your mouth is bleeding again.

LIBERTY *sits down at the table, her reserve cracked.* BRONTE *comforts her.*

LIBERTY

We fought last night but made up, and then I was at work for five hours, and when I came home he was totally pissed and it just started all over again. He thinks I'm having an affair.

BRONTE

What!

LIBERTY

Because I've been right off sex since I got pregnant—I'm so sick I can't believe it!

BRONTE

Why haven't you told him then?

LIBERTY

I don't know. I was going to tell him last night. It's my fault, I forgot to take the pill.

BRONTE

It's all your fault, isn't it?

LIBERTY

Will you hate him for me? If I can't manage it?

BRONTE

It would be better if you did it.

LIBERTY

Are you going to take me to the doctor's or not?

BRONTE

Yeah. Come on.

LIBERTY

You hate him, don't you? Why can't I hate him?

BRONTE

Come on.

LIBERTY

I'm sorry Bronte, about what I said. I'm so tired.

BRONTE

SShhh. Forget it. I'll look after you.

LIBERTY

Will you go and see if Dan's all right?

BRONTE

Let's just take care of you first.

LIBERTY *is stalling.*

BRONTE

What's wrong now?

LIBERTY

Nothing. I was just wondering, do you think we choose our own endings?

BRONTE

No. We choose beginnings. Let's go.

LIBERTY *remains seated and freezes.*

BRONTE

She didn't leave him. Not this time. She left a few years later, though, a few miscarriages later. When she discovered he was having an affair. It's funny what kind of things people get insulted by, isn't it? They're still married. Oh, yes, I almost forgot—I live with Dan now, up at the lake. Well, you know. When he comes back from his women, from his wanderings, he brings the dampness of the lake with him, and wraps me in his fog. A man like him, you have to love him with your eyes half closed. You don't want to see everything. Otherwise I might look across the lake to where Liberty has gone. But I don't dream of escape, I dream of death. Last night I had this dream. We were in bed. It was storming outside and I couldn't see anything but black wind. As I fell asleep I felt Dan's heavy hands around my throat. I was choking, but when I touched them to struggle I couldn't help thinking how beautiful they were. I wanted to open my eyes to see if I was still there, but I couldn't. Hours later when I woke up he was sleeping peacefully beside me and I went straight to the mirror to check that I was still alive. I am. But there were small red marks around my neck, like a ruby necklace made of globules of blood. No finger marks. 'Have I done this to myself?', I thought.

BRONTE *and* LIBERTY *exit.*

THE END

Moss

Characters

CELESTE, *the reindeer.*
DIANA, *her older sister.*
MARK, *Diana's husband.*
CARVER, *their friend.*

Set

A city; a house in the country; a forest.

Scene 1

The city. MARK *and* DIANA *are asleep. The stillness is transformed at first by a gentle breeze, and then by haunting voices.*

VOICES
Diana Diana Diana Diana Diana.

Every time DIANA *stirs the voices retreat, or cease, beginning again when she settles. The wind is now wilder and blowing the curtains strongly. This noise is gradually overwhelmed by the sound of hooves, moving with haste and panic. Accompanying this sound is a visual of a herd of furious reindeers, spinning around the theatre space, magnifying what* DIANA *is experiencing in her dream. As these shadows play, a figure appears in the window. It is* CELESTE.

CELESTE

Diana.

DIANA *sits bolt upright. There is a moment of silence and stillness. The storm climaxes.* CELESTE *leaps outside.* DIANA *screams.* MARK *calms* DIANA.

DIANA

Bad dream.

MARK

I love you.

MARK *sleeps.* DIANA *moves to the window and watches the gentle rain falling.*

Scene 2

The city, night. DIANA, MARK, CARVER *and* CELESTE *are together, drinking, and laughing loudly. Music is playing until* CELESTE *snaps her fingers, when it stops abruptly. The others freeze as* CELESTE *approaches the audience.*

CELESTE

We all make mistakes. Some people just keep on making them. Like we did, playing the same old games. 'Carver loves Diana loves Mark loves Celeste' and every variation thereof, year after year. I'd had enough. I was out of there. [*Pause*] Look at us—we all seem so much in love, so very happy.

CELESTE *breaks the freeze. She sits with the others silently, drinking diligently.*

CARVER

Listen to me, you shithead.

MARK

'Shithead'. A brilliant adjective from a superior mind.

DI

Noun, darling, it was a very correct proper noun.

MARK

Fuck off Di.

DI

You both give me the shits. I'm going to bed. Thanks for another riveting evening, Carver. Your wife's problems are simply fascinating.

She kisses them all goodnight. CARVER *fights off her affection.*

CARVER

Fuck you then.

DI

Oh, cheer up.

DI *goes to bed.*

MARK

Go home and insult your own wife, Carver. You're boring.

CARVER

Fuck you too.

MARK

Goodnight!

CARVER *exits.* CELESTE *stands as if to go after him then sits, pours more wine for them both, and resumes drinking.*

MARK

Arsehole.

MARK *sighs deeply. This has been a typical evening. Blackout.*

Scene 3

The city, later that night.

DI

I want to go on the program.

MARK

Di, if you'd just wait until / later maybe things . . .

DI

/1No. No more waiting. We've been married nine years Mark. Nine /Fucking years.

MARK

/Alright.

DI

No more waiting.

MARK

We'll talk about it. I promise.

DI

No. No more talk.

The phone rings. MARK *answers.*

DI

You are not going in to work Mark. No way.

MARK

Hello. Yes. No. / She's asleep.

DI

/ Who is it?

MARK

What? / How?

DI

/ Is it Carver? Typical. Drunken remorse in the wee hours.

MARK *gestures to* DI *to shut up.*

MARK

[*Silence*] Just hang in there, mate. / No problem.

DI

/ Oh god.

MARK

I'll see you soon. OK.

DI

What.

MARK

It was Carver.

DI

Really.

MARK

Diana . . .

DI

He can deal with it on his own.

MARK

Di. Karen's dead.

DI

Dead?

MARK

Suicide.

DI

I see. Is he alone?

MARK

Yes. Alone.

DI

[*Pause*] Well. That reduces the weekend to a perfect foursome.

The window bursts open. A large shadow of a deer falls across the room.

MARK

What the fuck has happened here? We're meant to be friends.

DI *reclines in bed, lighting up a cigarette.*

Scene 4

The city, a flashback to many years earlier. CARVER *is waiting in a bar, drinking.* MARK *enters, with a beer in each hand.*

CARVER

Mark, matey, how's it going.

MARK

Carver, G'day. Thanks for waiting.

CARVER

It's been a pure delight. I could watch that red-headed barmaid over there pull beers for hours.

MARK

Karen ?

CARVER

She's a bit of alright.

MARK

She's as thick as two planks.

CARVER

I wasn't planning on holding a conversation with her, mate. [*Pause*] Swanko drinking hole you've got here.

MARK

Got to belong to the right clubs to get ahead.

CARVER

I didn't know you played golf.

MARK

I don't.

CARVER

God you're a poncy bastard. Nice barmaids though. [*Pause*]

MARK

How's work?

CARVER

Oh. You know.

MARK

Surf's up is it?

CARVER

Yeah. Has been for a while. So. Been up to any mischief lately?

MARK

Not much. Aside from looking for a good divorce lawyer.

CARVER

You've only been married a minute.

MARK

Six months.

CARVER

Fucking great party. Are you serious?

MARK

I leaf through the yellow pages waiting for her to come home, looking under 'B' for barristers.

CARVER

Lighten up. She used to make me look under 'F'.

MARK

Florists?

CARVER

Funeral Directors.

MARK

Women.

CARVER

[*Raising his glass*] To women!

MARK

To women.

They toast, then walk to separate upstage positions, talking to the audience. The flashback is over.

CARVER

We used to be great friends, / I'd never known anyone like him.

MARK

/ I'd never known anyone like him. Carver was a good friend to me. / A mate.

CARVER

/ A mate, he was. Never gave me a hard time. I was happy to see Di safe. / But then things went wrong.

MARK

/ But then things went wrong. Sour. / Different lives, you know.

CARVER

/ Different lives, you know, we have completely different values. I made an effort, you know, / because of Di.

MARK

/ Because of Di, because / I loved her, we all made an effort.

CARVER

/ I loved her.

MARK

That was the end of that conversation. Enough of me and my marital problems. Mates don't need to talk about shit like that. We talked about the footy instead. I went home. Carver went home with the barmaid. These days we don't even talk about the footy.

CARVER *and* MARK *walk towards each other.*

MARK & CARVER

These days, when we meet, you know . . .

CARVER *and* MARK *meet centre stage, smile and shake hands forcefully, with a bit of back slapping.*

CARVER & MARK

Maaate!

They break their contact, take a step back, glaring at each other.

CARVER & MARK

... things are a bit ...

MARK

... shall we say ...

CARVER & MARK

... strained.

MARK *and* CARVER *exit.*

Scene 5

The city, a few days after KAREN*'s death.* CELESTE *and* DIANA *are shopping for clothes in an expensive boutique.* DIANA *is trying things on and coming out to look in the mirrors during their whole conversation.* CELESTE *chain smokes.*

DI

Oh come on. I need some help.

CELESTE

Have you tried sex?

DI

This dress has an atrocious cut.

CELESTE

It sucks. [*Silence*] Are you going to leave him?

DI

[*Silence*] Are you? Leaving. Is that what this is all about. You'd tell me / wouldn't you, before you went away anywhere.

CELESTE

/ Of course, of course I'd tell you. I am telling you. There. I've told you.

DI

This would look good on you. [*Pause*] Bit sudden, your decision. Are you serious? Where are you going?

CELESTE

Come with me, Di.

DI

I can't.

CELESTE

He'll live without you.

DI

[*Pause*] It's not Mark I'm worried about.

CELESTE

Oh. I see. That same old story.

DI

It's not what you think. God. I should've never talked him into marrying that dead bitch.

CELESTE

Well. He did. [*Pause*] I wish you wouldn't speak about Karen like that.

DI

He only bloody stayed with her because she kept threatening suicide.

CELESTE

I know.

DI

Karen shmaren, I've had enough of her. We are not responsible for her death, / nor is Carver. And I for one will not be held

CELESTE

/ We ignored her for years on end!

DI

responsible for Carver's 'feelings' towards me. Even if they did upset precious Karen.

CELESTE

Do you still love him?

DI

Oh for god's sake Celeste.

CELESTE

Do you?

DI

It was a long time ago, Celeste.

CELESTE

Tell me you don't want Carver.

DI

I don't want Carver.

CELESTE

Diana, I do have to go away. And I want you to come.

DI

I assume that you presume that I'll pay for your ticket. As per fucking usual.

CELESTE

What is wrong with you?

DI

Nothing! Everything. [*Silence*] Mark has sexual dreams about you.

CELESTE

[*Pause*] And what do you dream about?

DI

You. [*Pause*] So you will come this weekend?

CELESTE

OK.

DI

It'll be a great birthday party.

CELESTE

Farewell party.

DI

Come on.

DIANA *gathers her intended purchases together.* CELESTE *stops smoking.*

CELESTE

Di.

DI

Uhuh.

CELESTE

Do you think we're living our lives the right way?

DI

God. You really are getting old.

CELESTE

It's more than that.

DI

Karen made a bad decision.

CELESTE

That's not all.

DI

[*Pause*] You'll get over it Celeste. You just need some time. Abortions are tough.

CELESTE

I want my baby back.

DI

I want a lot of things back.

DI *goes to* CELESTE *and holds her.* CELESTE *starts to cry as heavy sounds of the city flood the stage.*

Scene 6

The city, early evening the next day. MARK *and* CARVER *are in their respective bathrooms, in towels, shaving. They concentrate on their toilet for a while, then talk to the audience.*

CARVER

[*Singing the refrain from an Angels' song*] 'Am I ever gonna see your face again, uh uh, uh uh, ah ah, I don't ever want to see your face again, no way, get fucked, fuck off'. [*Silence*] She said to me that she will always think of me with great affection.

MARK

Sweet woman of my youth, try as I do to get you out of my blood, you steal my love away, drop by drop.

CARVER

You don't know what woman I'm talking about, / do you?

MARK

/ Do you know what woman I'm talking about? That's just it. That's the problem. I've spent my whole life talking about women. Not to them.

CARVER

It was affection. A great affection.

MARK

Have you ever tried to talk to a woman? I've had more meaningful conversations with a record. A long stretch of road, even. My problem is that I'm a great deceiver. A woman once pushed my face into a mirror and said 'convince this, convince this person, because you sure as shit aren't fooling me'. Love. What? What does it mean. Well, I guess the lesson was meant to be about honesty. But I'm not stupid. I'm in fact extremely clever. I have since learnt to fool myself. Lies, lies. More fool me.

CARVER

Have you ever tried to talk to a woman? I've had more meaningful conversations with my mirror. More interesting, too. I'm convinced. My problem is I that always did get tongue-tied around women. I'm one of those what you'd call 'silent communicators'. Now, that's real nice. When we're both silent. Peaceful. Love. What? What is it? Do you know when a woman shuts up? When they listen most? When you're making love. I've learnt how to do that real good. Now that's a truthful communication. No more lies. You can't fool me.

Still talking to the audience.

CARVER

I only ever talked to my Dad about men shit. As a result I am an excellent bullshitter, and barbequer. I also do a good lawn. And I know a lot about 'sheilas'. God help me.

MARK

It was a great surprise for me to learn quite late in life that my friends were a bunch of fuckwits. I feel disappointed, because all of a sudden I realised: / I'm all alone.

CARVER

/ I'm all alone. She jumped, you know. Just jumped right out the fucking window.

MARK

It's not the same any more. / Nothing ever is.

CARVER

/ Nothing ever is. Like you think it is. That's a good lesson to learn. Yeah. / You don't know what you've got until it's gone.

MARK

/ You don't know what you've got until it's gone.

CARVER

Yeah.

They resume their toilet. DI *and* CELESTE *enter, each in their respective homes, and complete their travel preparations.* DI *is efficient.* CELESTE *can't decide on anything.*

DI

Mark. Mark, are you nearly ready in there? I'm packed, I packed you this morning, I've just got to clean my teeth then we can go. We should leave within five to seven minutes to collect Celeste. I've organised her to wait outside.

MARK

I'll be ready. Di?

DI

Yes.

MARK

Are you planning to relax this weekend?

She throws something at him and misses. He retaliates. Some hanky panky ensues until MARK *breaks off.*

MARK

By the way. I got the results.

DI

And?

MARK

I make lots of money but not much sperm. Apparently. That's how it is. I'm sorry.

DI

[*Comforting him*] Plan B is looking good then?

CELESTE *is waiting, and hums 'Rudolf the Red-nosed Reindeer' whilst powdering her nose. She finishes, and throws the compact away in disgust. She tips all her clothes out. She then picks up the phone and dials.* CARVER*'s phone rings.*

CARVER

Yellow. Hello. Hello. Who's there? Hello?

CELESTE *hangs up, then* CARVER.

CELESTE

Bye bye.

CELESTE *starts humming again.* DI *and* MARK *pick up suitcases and leave.* CELESTE *hurriedly writes a letter, then runs out.* CARVER *elaborately wraps a present.*

Scene 7

The house in the country, later that evening. DI, MARK *and* CELESTE *are sitting around singing. It's late, they have been there for some time.*

TOGETHER

'I asked my love / to take a walk / to take a walk / just a little walk . . . '

They start humming because they can't remember the words.

DI

How does that song end?

MARK

In tragedy. Like every love story this century.

CELESTE

Optimist.

MARK

Innocent.

DI

She stabbed him to death, didn't she, [*sings*] ' . . . down by the banks / of the Ohio'.

MARK

/ Told you so.

CELESTE

I'm not an innocent.

MARK

I hate to ruin your soufflé Celeste but you could easily be mistaken for Mary Poppins' best friend.

DI

Mark. Don't be cruel. I'm warning you.

MARK

Oh stop being so fucking unhappy all the time Di, it's really quite unsociable of you.

DI

Stop telling me how fucking unhappy I'm supposed to be. I am not unhappy.

MARK

You're sounding very convincing there, darling, keep it up.

DI

Oh shut up. I'm sick of your pithy summaries of my feelings. [*Pause*] If I want to fuck Carver I will. Stop fooling yourself that I'm only after his sperm.

CELESTE

Are you fucking Carver?

MARK

Yes. She is.

DI

I'm merely thinking about it.

CELESTE

Where is he anyway?

MARK

Grieving.

CELESTE *laughs.*

DI

What's so funny?

MARK

I think she's amused, darling, like I am. It's rather quaint, after all.

DI

You should be grateful, Mark, it's always an advantage to know your competition.

CELESTE

You two make me feel really sad. Really sad.

MARK

Carver's not competition. He's just . . .

DI

Fertile.

CELESTE

Leave my brother-in-law alone.

MARK

She'll never leave me alone. She'd never leave my bank account. Would you sweetheart?

DI

Don't.

CELESTE

It's easier than you might think Mark.

DI

What do you know? Everything's easy for you Celeste.

CELESTE

What?

DI

Easy enough. To get pregnant. To kill so lightly.

MARK

You can be such a complete cow sometimes Diana.

DI

Yes. I'm sorry sis.

CELESTE

You should get divorced, you two.

MARK

Nah. It's just that low tide feeling. It'll pass. Won't it darling?

CELESTE

Why don't you ever take me seriously?

DI

I happen to like the low tides in my life, Celeste.

CELESTE

That's because you spend them with Carver.

DI

You've had quite enough to drink sweetie, you're getting melancholic.

CELESTE

You never listen to me. What's the point?

DI

Don't sulk, baby, I'm too tired. I think I'll take my doomed self off to bed.

CELESTE

Don't go to bed yet, not now. / I was about to . . .

MARK

/ You should. Tomorrow's the big night after all.

DI

Yes

MARK

I'm not tired.

DI

Not like old hag-features here. Good night beloveds.

CELESTE

Goodnight then.

MARK

I'll be up soon.

DI *exits.* MARK *selects a book, taking his time.* CELESTE *watches him intently.*

MARK

How about a good night story?

CELESTE

I've never said anything to her.

MARK

I have no secrets from my wife.

CELESTE

And just what do you have from your wife, Mark?

MARK

Don't, Celeste, I'm on your side.

CELESTE

How long are you going to carry on with this shit?

MARK

Excuse me?

CELESTE

Pretending you love her. You've been looking at me all night long.

MARK

A second ago you were flirting with me.

CELESTE

A second ago! That was a century ago. I am testing you, do you understand?

MARK

Don't insult me.

CELESTE

Insult you? What about me? All my life I've been second in line in the 'try the sister' party game. Never first. It's time for me to lead the way for a change.

MARK

So you have been considering it. The idea. Us. Have you? [*Pause*] Don't bother. Don't answer. Fuck that's good wine. I managed to avoid this scene for the last eleven years only to be undone by a superior red.

CELESTE

So you don't count last Christmas? Or three years ago under the wattle tree at Mal's?

MARK

I must drink more than I think I do. You're a dangerous woman.

CELESTE

And you're gutless. You always were all talk, no action.

MARK

You've got nothing to lose.

CELESTE

You're right.

MARK

I think of you with the greatest respect and a burgeoning immoral love, and you spit on me. Fuck Celeste, what's a man got to do?

CELESTE

A man? Make Diana happy.

MARK

'Happy'? Would you like me to start walking on water while I'm at it?

He moves to touch her. CELESTE *puts up her hands in warning, he stops.*

CELESTE

No.

MARK

No. Right. Excuse me. I think I'll have to finish this conversation tomorrow. I have a sudden overwhelming desire to go and fuck my wife.

There is a loud knocking at the door.

MARK

Are you expecting anyone?

MARK *stands there while* CELESTE *opens the door.* CARVER *steps inside, carrying a duffel bag, a bottle of Vodka, and the present he was wrapping earlier.*

CARVER

Hi. I was just passing by.

MARK

Carver. Hello.

CARVER

Did you ever consider buying a beach house? It's fucking freezing up here.

CELESTE

Come in.

MARK

This is a surprise.

CARVER

Celeste.

CELESTE

Carver.

MARK

I thought you understood the rules mate.

CARVER

Di said if I needed . . . I thought that . . . well, I brought some vodka.

CELESTE

I was very sorry to hear about your wife Carver.

The three stand there until CELESTE *breaks and moves to* CARVER, *embracing him.*

MARK

Yes.

CARVER

There weren't many people at the funeral.

MARK

Yes. Well. Sorry. You understand.

CARVER

Yes. I do.

CELESTE

[*Silence*] Can I get you anything Carver?

MARK

We were just going to bed.

CARVER

No thanks Celeste.

MARK

Like I said . . .

CELESTE

Good night then. I'll see you in the morning.

MARK

Good night.

CARVER

Sleep tight.

CELESTE

Goodnight.

CELESTE *exits.*

MARK

You've got a hide.

CARVER

I haven't come to make trouble.

MARK

Pig's arse.

CARVER

How's Celeste?

MARK

Better than Karen.

CARVER

Listen fucknuckle, I was invited / remember? But I decided

MARK

/ Invited?

CARVER

against it because I know what a turd you are. / I only dropped

MARK

/ Did you say invited?

CARVER

by to leave this parcel here.

MARK

Parcel?

CARVER

Yeah. A brown paper package tied up with string.

CARVER *hands* MARK *the parcel, then puts his bags down, intending to stay.*

MARK

Thanks.

CARVER

It's for Celeste, gherkin brain.

MARK

Gherkin brain. Who do you hang out with, mate?

CARVER

Your wife, mostly. And yes, I was invited. Before you so kindly uninvited me and cancelled the weekend out of respect. For my grief. But I guess you changed your mind. Out of respect for Celeste—why spoil a good party? See that she gets her birthday present. Take care of her.

MARK

Don't play Mr Sensitive with me Carver. What's it to you anyway?

CARVER

More than you know mate. You'd better read this.

CARVER *hands* MARK *the letter that* CELESTE *had been writing.* MARK *doesn't read it.*

MARK

Fine example of a grieving husband you are. Can't even spend a weekend alone to mull over your life.

CARVER

Give us a break Mark.

MARK

[*Pause*] Are you OK?

CARVER

Just read the letter.

MARK

Why arrive out of the blue? So late?

CARVER

Oh, I had to wrap the present. Then I answered some condolence cards. Then I had a bit of a sob and then I thought about how you treat Di and then about how you both treat me in my time of great need. Then I got angry and decided to come, and by that time, by the time I packed and got to the station, well, hell, time just flies.

MARK

Carver it's against my nature to be nice to philistinic fuckwits but I do have a heart. / Seeing that you are my wife's dear friend, notice my

CARVER

/ Pumping pure shit.

MARK

emphasis on the word 'friend', and that you are emotionally disabled / due to your recent tragic past, and considering that you have

CARVER

/ Not for long, mate.

MARK

indeed travelled all this way, you might as well stay.

CARVER

You generous bastard.

MARK

My generosity is a peculiar breed, loaded heavy with the obligation of return.

CARVER

I told you, I brought some vodka.

MARK

Stay away from my wife. This is my territory mate.

CARVER

I've got different plans, mate. Believe me.

Scene 8

The country house, the next morning. CELESTE *is reading when* DI *enters.*

DI

Morning.

CELESTE

Morning.

DI

Any good?

CELESTE

This woman's been standing on the edge of the lake for the last nine pages trying to summon up the courage to take the plunge.

DI

Riveting.

CELESTE

Then finally being in the air is more painful than being in the water. She bends and pushes herself reluctantly into the lake.

DI

What are you reading that depressing crap for?

CELESTE

It's a feminist classic.

DI

God help us. Happy Birthday baby.

The sisters embrace, then CELESTE *moves away from* DIANA *to a position of dominance.*

CELESTE

Thanks.

DI

How do you feel?

CELESTE

Like you're trying to set me up with Carver.

DI

I swear to you, Celeste, I didn't know he was coming. We cancelled him.

CELESTE

Sure.

DI

I'm in fact quite pissed off at / him because Mark's pissed off and that pisses

CELESTE

/ You look angry.

DI

me off and I really wanted this to be a perfect escape / for all of

CELESTE

/ But then, you're such a performer.

DI

us. Carver, bless his punctured psyche, has barged in uninvited where he was not wanted. I did not plan this, this is not my organisational style.

CELESTE

And what is your style?

DI

Have a heart, Celeste, don't you just cry when you look at him?

CELESTE

No.

DI

Oh come on. I break the man's heart by marrying someone he introduced me to, someone who smelt like my future, / and then because I

CELESTE

/ You were wrong there!

DI

rely on his large lips around my big heart to keep me alive, I couldn't let him go. / Then I push him into the arms of a

CELESTE

/ You've never tried.

DI

psychopathic bitch just so I can breathe, so I can touch my husband and myself with our own promise, and then she kills herself. / I'm responsible for his grief, Celeste. I am.

CELESTE

/ Crying shame.

DI

I hate myself.

CELESTE

How on earth do you find the time.

DI

I don't understand your bitch, Celeste. One minute you're criticising me for not paying you enough attention and whinging about me inviting Carver, which I didn't, and the next you're going on about me neglecting him. Make up your mind.

CELESTE

Why treat Mark and Carver like you do? It's not their fault that you're addicted to them. To all this shit.

DI

Addicted! Oh come on. If anything it's the other way around.

CELESTE

No? Then leave. Leave them both.

DI

I love them Celeste. [*Pause*] And besides, where would I go?

CELESTE

You could come with me.

DI

And just where are you going?

CELESTE

Away.

DI

What a perfect plan. I'll go and pack, shall I? [*Pause*] You've run away from everything all your life. That's exactly why your life is shit.

CELESTE

And yours is an endless rose garden.

DI

[*Pause*] I'm sorry.

CELESTE

Don't. Fight. With. Me.

DI

I'll make it up to you, if there's something I said then . . .

CELESTE

It's everything you, said, actually. And more.

DI

Celeste?

CELESTE

More than I can stand.

DI

You're frightening me. What's wrong.

CELESTE

You don't know, do you?

DI

What?

CELESTE

What I'm upset about.

DI

What is it?

CELESTE

You really don't know.

DI

No.

CELESTE *moves back to an intimate position with* DIANA.

CELESTE

That guy I told you about.

DI

The one who . . .

It gradually dawns on DI *that* CELESTE *is talking about* CARVER.

DI

You're kidding? It was Carver? You're serious. [*Pause*] You're not in love with him?

CELESTE

He's not my man to love.

DI

Celeste, I . . . I don't know what to say. He's not mine either.

CELESTE

Try and tell Karen that.

DI

Why didn't you tell me?

CELESTE

What difference would it have made?

DI

Difference!

CELESTE

Yes, difference.

DI

None, I suppose. I could have protected you. I could . . . kick him out now. If you want.

CELESTE

No. It's not your fault he came. I just want to know what he's doing here.

DI

I wish you'd told me, Celeste. And I can't believe Carver didn't tell me. The bastard.

CELESTE

I didn't tell anyone. I was ashamed.

DI

Why?

CELESTE

Married. He was so married.

DI

My husband is married. Didn't he tell you that?

CELESTE

This is absurd.

Silence

DI

So how long did it go on?

CELESTE

Di. Don't. / Listen to me.

DI

/ Did Karen ever find out?

CELESTE

I don't know. I stopped seeing Carver at the end of last summer. Ages before . . . [*Silence*]

DI

It was serious then. A long time.

CELESTE

I feel responsible. About Karen. I think she did find out. I . . . I liked her a lot.

DI

She was no great friend of mine, I can assure you.

CELESTE

I know. So did she—you know she's always known about you and Carver.

DI

Stupid bitch.

Silence

DI

You and Carver made a baby.

Silence

CELESTE

Yes.

DI

You told me it was from a one night stand.

CELESTE

My whole life feels like a one night stand. Even when it lasts for years.

DI

You lied to me.

CELESTE

It's over.

DI

Why? Why didn't you tell me?

CELESTE

I never had anything worth lying about before.

DI

Do you still love him?

CELESTE

Where are the boys?

DI

Gone to get the papers do you still love him? I need to know.

CELESTE

I thought you said it didn't make any difference.

DI

Maybe I lied.

CELESTE

What matters is getting through this weekend and coming out the other side intact. I do have manners, I won't spoil you're precious holiday, I won't fuck your husband or your boyfriend, both of whom you profess not to care about, and I won't embarrass you by refusing to eat your traditionally pathetic attempt at a birthday cake. Just leave me alone and I'll deal with it.

DI

[*Pause*] Sorry. Sorry.

CELESTE

I'm sorry I never told you. I was frightened.

DI

Of me?

CELESTE

Of losing you.

CELESTE *and* DI *embrace.*

DI

Celeste . . . Look. I've been thinking. About what you said to me last night.

CARVER *and* MARK *enter from outside and take off their heavy coats and boots.*

DI

We'll talk later.

CELESTE

No!

MARK

Yoohoo, birthday girl, look what we've brought for you.

He has brought flowers, CARVER *has more alcohol.* CELESTE *and* DI *sit up, united on the couch.* DI *glares at* CARVER.

CARVER.

It's freezing out there! It was a bloody cold walk all the way from the train station at midnight.

DI

You should have phoned.

CARVER

I wanted to surprise you.

DI

It worked.

MARK

So. What are we doing today people?

CARVER

Let's eat, I'm starving.

MARK

Good idea.

MARK *waits for someone to make lunch.* MARK *realises that no one will get up except him, he exits.*

DI

Celeste and I have been having a little sisterly talk Carver.

CARVER

And.

DI

And.

She walks up to him and slaps him hard.

CARVER

Are you over it then?

DI

I expect that nothing more will be said on this subject. You have both hurt each other badly, the two people who I love most in the world. Now let's all behave and enjoy the day.

CARVER

You're a fucking weird woman Diana.

CELESTE

Leave her alone.

DI

I am not alone in my weirdness, Carver. You obviously didn't know my sister too well. It's a family trait. We pride ourselves in it. I'm sorry about this shoddy start to your birthday darling, let's begin again.

CELESTE

No, I'm sorry.

MARK *returns with coffee.*

MARK

Coffee's ready. What's she making you feel guilty about now Celeste?

CELESTE

Nothing.

DI *deliberately spills her coffee on* CARVER.

DI

Sorry.

MARK

Are you OK?

CARVER

Fuck knows. We're in the middle of a forest with the two crazy witch sisters.

MARK

Get used to it.

DI

Let's change the subject.

MARK

Shall we do the weather?

CARVER

It looks like more snow.

DI

Could I have some more coffee. Please. [*She holds her cup out, both men go to get it*] Mark.

CELESTE

I'll get it.

MARK

And I'll get some food organised so we can get going on that walk. Preferably sometime before darkness descends.

CELESTE *and* MARK *exit. Nothing is said for a while.*

CARVER

I do think it's gonna snow.

DI

I think it's 'gonna snow' and storm and rage and sleet pig's swill down on our ugly heads, and the terror of the wilderness will make our hearts bleed mud while wolves gnaw our frozen feet.

CARVER

You can be a histrionic bitch sometimes Diana.

DI

You haven't seen the half of it.

Scene 9

The forest, later that afternoon. CARVER *is alone in a clearing, taking time to tie his boots. The voices of* CELESTE, DI *and* MARK *are heard, as though the trees are speaking to him.* CARVER *can hear them but tries to ignore them.*

MARK

The forest is a dangerous place.

CELESTE

Did you push her or did she jump, Carver? You always said to me, 'if only I wasn't married'.

DI

If only.

MARK

A dangerous place indeed. People die out here.

DI

Did you push her or did she jump? You pushed her, didn't you.

MARK

It would be possible for you to lose your way and never return.

DI

If only. / If only.

CELESTE

/ If only you had been true. Now every one is blue.

MARK

And it's a punishing experience, / trying to find your way.

DI

/You threatened me. That you'd do it.

MARK

I'm here to tell you that our respect for animals is not reciprocated. They fear us, hate us, they will kill us. There is no / respect.

CELESTE

/ Respect. The same respect I once gave you I now save for me.

MARK

You are the enemy in their eyes.

CELESTE

They are not used to human kindness.

MARK

That's the problem, animals do not appreciate your philanthropy, / and therein lies the danger.

CELESTE

/ And therein lies the danger. Why are men frightened of women?

MARK

Fear them. Or kill them. Keep your respect to yourself, it is no weapon in the wilderness.

CELESTE

So / watch out.

DI

/ Watch out.

CELESTE, DI and MARK are waiting some distance from CARVER.

MARK

What's keeping the incredible hulk?

CELESTE

This is fantastic out here. I don't know, he's having some problems with his boots.

MARK

Too big for them, no doubt.

DI

It'll be dark soon. I'd better check on what's holding him up.

CELESTE

Those clouds look great.

DI

They look like snow. I'll go and find Carver.

MARK

We'll wait right here. Don't get lost.

DI

I won't. Go on, go home and light the fire.

She leaves them.

CELESTE

So. / It's time we . . .

MARK

/ It's time we . . . Sorry.

CELESTE

Don't be.

MARK

I don't know if you can understand this. I think I have to leave Diana. To let her go.

CELESTE

Which then?

MARK

What?

CELESTE

Leave, or let her go.

MARK

I . . .

CELESTE

I think, Mark, the decision has already been made. For you.

MARK

Oh. Good. That's good. What then? . . . Carver?

CELESTE

No. Nothing like that. I . . . she's coming away with me.

MARK

What?

CELESTE

What's wrong?

MARK

Nothing. Just . . . well. All those years. I love her Celeste.

CELESTE

I know. But not enough.

MARK

No. He's a hard man to compete with. Carver.

CELESTE

Yes. So is that why you waste half your life chasing after me?

MARK

No. No. I just . . . I . . . Well to tell you the truth Celeste you remind me of someone I used to know.

CELESTE

Heard that one before.

Silence

MARK

So. The little sister is turning . . . how old is it? What's you big birthday wish, then?

CELESTE

Really?

MARK

Really.

CELESTE

I'd like to go to sleep and wake up as someone else.

MARK

Ah. The forest is a dangerous place. Full of magic. Don't wish too hard.

They've been walking. They come upon DI *and* CARVER *having sex.*

Scene 10

The country house, later that night. The two men are setting the table for the birthday dinner. They are wearing party headpieces, MARK *has elephant ears, and* CARVER *wears stag horns.*

CARVER

Just what is your problem?

MARK

Your horns are lopsided.

CARVER

You're finished mate.

MARK

Not nearly.

DI

[*Enters*] Stop it, the both of you. Do you hear me? Now finish setting this fucking table, and light those candles. If you don't conduct yourselves with the charm and deadly attraction that you are both capable of, then you can eat in the garage. Celeste and I have better things to talk about. I'm sure. Excuse me, the bouillabaisse beckons.

DI *exits. The men work in silence.* CARVER *accidentally breaks a glass.*

CARVER

Shit. Sorry.

MARK

Really.

CARVER

Hey, it was an accident.

MARK

Was it?

CARVER

I said I'm sorry.

MARK

Your motor skills are about as impeccable as your manners. Or your timing for that matter. Why now, why this weekend? We could have sorted things out ourselves without this nauseous opera that you're dragging us through.

CARVER

Maybe. I shouldn't have come.

MARK

But you did. Come.

CARVER

I thought... everything... was OK. I didn't think you'd mind.

MARK

God you're a confident bastard.

CARVER

That's why you like me.

MARK

Who says I like you.

DI *enters carrying a cauldron.*

CARVER

But you don't mind, do you?

DI

Mind what? Where's Celeste, this is ready.

CARVER

You don't give a shit.

DI

Who doesn't give a shit about what? Restore your festive mood please gentlemen. We're all friends here. Remember.

MARK

No one. Gives a shit about anything.

CARVER

That's it. That's just it. It's nothing to you.

DI

What's going on?

MARK

I'll call Celeste.

CARVER

Mr calm, Mr cool, Mr fool, Mr 'this all means nothing to me'. Your 'nothing', your neglect, gave me licence to love Diana.

DI

Carver. Does this have to happen / right now?

CARVER

/ You're no better. You care even less about yourself than he does.

MARK

It's not me who doesn't care. I'd say it's you, Carver, to whom all this means 'nothing'. I am the one who will suffer most.

DI

For fuck's sake Mark.

MARK

Shut up.

CARVER

You shut up, arsehole.

MARK

About what, particularly? About you screwing my wife, or about you killing your wife?

CARVER

Take that back.

DI

I forgot the serving spoon.

DI *goes to leave, but is grabbed by* CARVER.

CARVER

Stay.

DI

Well. I can see you two have absolutely no respect for the fact that I've been slaving in the kitchen all afternoon. To create a perfect dinner, and now all you care about is having a discussion about who has license over me. The fucking turkey in the oven has more license over me / than either of you.

CARVER

/ Listen. To me.

MARK

Let her go Carver.

CARVER *releases* DI *and moves to* MARK.

DI

Come on, Carver, he didn't mean it. About Karen. Did you Mark?

CARVER

You have no idea what went on between me and my wife. I loved her.

MARK *laughs in his face.* CARVER *punches him.*

CARVER

You have no idea what love is.

DI

Carver.

CARVER

Or you either. But shit I had some fun finding that out, didn't I? Didn't we?

DI *goes to leave again.* CARVER *grabs her.* CELESTE *enters.*

DI

Just leave things alone Carver.

During this speech CELESTE *paces the room, looking for exits.*

CARVER

You think you can walk away from everything? From this man lying here on the ground who loves you so much he'd drink your blood? From me? We are friends, aren't we? We must be. That's why you let me walk around like a lonely giant with bad breath all these years, isn't it, fucking anything, anybody that would give me a bit of relief from my completely fucked up life, which has been an endless source of amusement to you. Let me tell you something. Even if I could have read Karen's mind maybe I would've let her jump anyway, otherwise she would have been ruining your fucking dinner parties for the next three decades with her disappointment. And I bet she's in a better place right now than any of us will ever even glimpse because she was a good woman, so fucking good, and we're just full of rust. So don't you dare tell me to leave things alone.

DI

Carver . . .

CARVER

Castrator.

DI

I'm sorry.

CARVER

Class traitor.

DI

I'm sorry about Karen.

CARVER

I'm sorry about everything.

MARK

We are your friends Carver. We are.

CARVER

Fuck friends.

He exits, DI *follows.*

CELESTE

OK. That's it.

MARK *ignores her and follows the others.*

VOICES

Come with me. Come with me. Come with me.

CELESTE

Yes.

CELESTE *undresses while she sings.*

CELESTE

'It is the evening of the day / I sit and watch the children play / smiling voices I can see / but not for me/ I sit and watch / as tears go by . . .'

Naked, she exits with determination, chanting:

CELESTE
Not for me. Not for me. Not for me.

Scene 11

The country house, the next morning. CARVER, DI *and* MARK *are eating breakfast.*

CARVER
She's lucky to be alive.

MARK
What on earth possessed her to go walking in a snow storm?

CARVER
Naked.

DI
The doctor reckons the hypothermia really knocked her around. Poor kid.

MARK
She looked shocking.

DI
She'll be OK.

MARK
I hope so.

CARVER
She's tough. She can handle anything.

DI
Even the butcher's knife.

CARVER

So it seems.

MARK

Why did she do it? What on earth possessed her?

CARVER

It wasn't exactly the best birthday party in the world.

DI

We bored her, we ignored her, we sawed her in half with our cynicism, who wouldn't rather take a hike in a blizzard.

CARVER

Right. That's it. Let's sort / this out . . .

DI

/ No. That is not it. Not by a long shot.

MARK

You are both giving me indigestion.

DI

Here we go again, talking about us. 'Us, us, us'. My sister nearly died last night and all you two are interested in is who's going to be sharing my electric blanket with me for the rest of my life. It's just occurred to me, I don't like either of you very much.

MARK

You're under a lot of stress, we can / talk about it later.

DI

/ Yes I am under a lot of stress, I'm under a lot of stress because I've been under a lot of men. Under a lot of blankets, under a lot of tables, under a lot of trees, under a lot of stars. Come to think about it, I never could locate the stars. You blocked my vision. It's entirely unfair. The both of you have spent the best years of your lives enjoying the reflection of the stars in my eyes while I was busy trying to seize a clear view of them. Through you, through your bulk. All that fucking, and for what? Tell me. No, don't test my tolerance, I'll tell you. I'll tell you! 'Me me me', 'It, it, it', 'us, us, us', 'fuck, fuck, fuck' until I'm moonstruck with my own emptiness. I am so empty. You. Both. Make. Me. Feel. So. Empty.

MARK

Pass the salt.

DI *throws the salt at* MARK. CARVER *picks it up.*

DI

You bastard.

CELESTE *enters in a dressing gown.*

DI

It's over.

CELESTE

Good morning, good morning, good morning. Oh, you shouldn't have! Scrambled eggs, my favourite.

DI

Celeste, you shouldn't be out of bed.

CELESTE

I feel perfectly fine. I feel . . . thrilled!

MARK

Something to eat?

CELESTE

Yes please, I'm famished. I need my energy, too, for the journey.

DI

We don't have to leave today, / if you like

MARK

/ If you like I can stay up here with you. I want to.

DI

we can stay up here and have a real holiday. I can take some time off, take care of you. I will. Celeste. We all owe you an apology for last night.

CELESTE

Last night? It was the best night of my life.

CARVER

Here's some . . .

CARVER *is entranced by* CELESTE*'s hands, and pauses in handing her some cutlery.*

MARK

Cutlery, Carver, forks and knives are called cutlery.

CARVER

You prick. What's that on your hands Celeste.

CELESTE

Moss stains. Aren't they pretty. I was digging for Moss last night.

DI

Are you certain that you wouldn't rather eat in bed?

CELESTE

No, never. Bon appetit!

CELESTE *buries her head in her scrambled eggs and eats ravenously. Upon rising, she is perturbed to find the others looking shocked.*

DI

Your cutlery, Celeste. You forgot your cutlery.

CELESTE

I . . . I'm sorry. I didn't think you'd mind. You see, I can't hold a fork and knife any more. Not with these.

DI

With what?

CELESTE

These!

She holds up her hands for all to see.

CELESTE

My new hooves. Aren't they fabulous?

CARVER

Awe inspiring.

MARK

[*Joking*] Hooves?

DI

[*Worried, recalling her dream*] Hooves?

CELESTE

Didn't I tell you last night when I came home? About my hooves, about . . .

DI

Mark. Call the doctor please.

CELESTE

I don't need a doctor, Diana. I do need a bit of scratch though—no finger nails!—where I can feel my tail trying to break out. A tail, fancy that! Do you mind?

CARVER

Tell us Celeste? What happened last night?

CELESTE

Well. I met this doe and her baby while I was out walking. We hit it off, and seeing as things haven't been working out all that well here, I've decided, basically, to go and live in the forest. For a while. She promised to teach me everything. She can tell me where my baby went, so that will be fantastic, to find out, don't you think? Only catch is I had to agree to wear this disguise, she warned me that the change could be a bit painful, but so far, so good.

DI

Disguise.

CELESTE

More of a costume, really. To protect me in the forest. A reindeer outfit.

MARK

A reindeer outfit.

CELESTE

Yes. And this is the beginning, my hooves. They were there when I woke up. Woops, there goes my tail, pop! This feels great. Rather fashionable this bone colour, this winter. They should call it 'hoof white'.

DI

[*Seriously worried*] Call the doctor Mark. Celeste ... Celeste ...

CARVER

So let me get this straight. You and this reindeer got together last night in the middle of a snow storm / and she talked you into going to live

CELESTE

It was divine.

CARVER

with her / and you thought, what the heck, I might as well, and

CELESTE

/ snort snort chuffle.

CARVER

the only bummer was, now here's the tough part of the deal, that you had to agree to turn into a reindeer.

CELESTE

[*Giving a snorty laugh*] I can't tell you how happy I am.

CARVER

Would any one else like a joint?

DI

You have egg on your chin.

MARK

So your wish came true.

DI

What wish?

CELESTE

It's almost unbelievable isn't it?

MARK

To wake up as a different person.

CARVER

How about some Bloody Mary's then?

DI

Shut up. Sit down. Stop this. All of you. Stop this right now.

CELESTE

Ah, I can feel my ears unfurling. Oohh, / they're itchy too.

DI

Mark, oh my god. My dream . . .

CARVER

Are you OK? / Are you?

CELESTE

/ Better rush, I have to get there before I forget the way. I don't fancy being stuck here with you lot, three hunters and a virgin / reindeer.

CARVER

/ Virgin?

CELESTE

Best be off.

DI

Celeste. I've had enough. You're frightening me.

CELESTE

No, Diana, you haven't had enough. I have. You stay here and think about it until I can gather my strength to return for you. When I find my baby she'll need the both of us to suckle, after all this dry time. I'm not sure how long I'll be gone, how long it will take, but I'll be back for you as soon as I can. I'm late now. Do you mind if I borrow the car? Goodbye.

CELESTE *runs out. Sound of car starting up.* MARK *makes to go after her.*

CARVER

Let her go. Mark.

DI

Stop her.

CARVER

She needs you Diana.

DI

I . . . but . . .

MARK

Fuck you. Fuck the both of you.

MARK *follows* CELESTE. *Sound of motorbike.*

CARVER

What now Di? Looks like it's just you and me.

Scene 12

The forest, one year later. CARVER *and* DI *are having a picnic in a forest clearing.*

CARVER

Mark really was a wanker. I always thought that.

DI

You promised Carver.

CARVER

Hey, hey, don't be like that. Look, I'm sorry. Please, Di.

CELESTE *enters but throughout the scene* CARVER *and* DI *are oblivious to her presence. She is in full reindeer costume/makeup.*

DI

You promised we wouldn't talk about them. We made a deal.

CARVER

A deal's a deal [*silence*].

CELESTE

Nothing was louder than the hush sleeping in her blood after I went away. Whereas my heart was pumping peace all around my body.

DI

A year today/ since I last

CARVER

/ Tonight. A year tonight.

DI

saw you. / Do you realise

CARVER

/ Long time no see.

DI

how hard it was for me to not see you?/ I almost gave in.

CARVER

/It was your idea.

DI

So many times. But I had to get over it on my own / otherwise

CARVER

/ I know how that feels.

DI

How could I know? How could I ever know?

CARVER

And now you know.

DI

You're looking good Carver.

CARVER

I missed you. You're the cruellest bitch who ever lived.

DI

Exile is good for the soul.

CELESTE

Come with me.

CARVER

I'm glad you enjoyed it.

DI

I missed you too.

CARVER

Tell me straight Di. You wanted space, you've had it. Don't make me sit through an uncomfortable meal chit-fucking-chatting if you're just gonna tell me to piss off at the end.

CELESTE

That night, my birthday, I stood in the empty house. And I could feel all that warm blood crumbling useless from my womb. And I could hear the tragedy of all our lives fluting up the chimney, and then I thought of the perfect silence that I would meet outside in the snow. Of what might be possible if I could reinvent myself. And I left.

CARVER

Nothing's standing in your way now, Di. They're both gone.

DI

Yeah.

CARVER

Try it my way. For once. I love you.

DI

Did you . . . find out anything?

CARVER

Yeah. I love life. More than lots of people we know. Knew.

DI

I might be prepared to give it / one more chance.

CARVER

/ Prepared?

DI

If you are. Prepared.

CARVER

What do you think I am, a piece of meat you've been marinating for twelve months?

DI

Oh Carver.

CARVER

Come on Di.

CELESTE

All of us had at one time or another wanted to devour each other. Eat me. Eat me.

DI

Maybe the time has come, Carver, to compromise. To make some concessions.

CARVER

Don't you talk about concessions to me Diana. I'm all concessioned out, to tell you the truth.

DI

I was talking about me, Carver.

CARVER

Here's two airline tickets.

CELESTE

'Take, eat: this is my body.'

CARVER

Come with me, Diana. I'm only going to ask you once [*pause*].

DI

We need to talk about it. About Celeste.

CARVER

Look. She's probably in New York or somewhere having a great time. But I think if any one could really turn into a reindeer, Celeste could.

DI

I think . . . I need to know.

CARVER

About Mark?

DI

No. Poor Mark.

CARVER

Gutless prick.

CELESTE

Say what you have to say and leave. It's time.

CARVER *packs up the picnic.*

DI

[*To the audience*] Once upon a time my mother left me. Then my husband and my sister. Somewhere I think I left myself. Perhaps I'm lying down in some sand dune somewhere. And now. My god I've never met a man who tried so hard to make you love him. He deserves what he seeks, love. He won't find that with me, will he? I'm so brittle, I want to lie forever in a field of moss. I need a century to heal.

DI *returns to* CARVER *and allows him to embrace her. They talk to the audience.*

CARVER

Ok. I'm still trying, but I'm not sure that there's enough time. I could marry Diana and fuck her sweetly, that's what counts, and dream of babies that I must never touch because I am the long time spoiler of the universe, the lonely fucked up warrior. I have forgotten joy in the desperate process of passing it on, and the sad thing is, thinking about it, I guess I've always been defined by my hunger. To love. To love. I just want some peace.

DI

Ok, I'm still the good side of being too old. There's time. We have to make what amends we can. That's what counts, isn't it? I'm a good woman. I am childless. I am alone. I am divorced. There's something wrong with me, I'm not happy at all, I have forgotten joy. I should be satisfied, I could be. I'm not at all, and now, thinking about it, I have always been defined by my hunger. For love. For love. I just want some peace.

They stand, staring at each other.

CELESTE

In the end there were no words—had there ever been words? But I will always call, somehow, for you to follow.

CELESTE *exits.*

DI

Carver.

CARVER

Diana.

DI

The way we love each other, it's wrong.

CARVER

Yeah. It's great isn't it.

DI

I missed you so much.

CARVER

[*Pause*] Diana.

CARVER *holds out his hand to* DIANA

DI

Where are you going?

CARVER

I don't know. Coming?

DIANA *looks at him. It begins to snow. Shadows and the noise of a herd of reindeer crowd the stage. Snow. Silence.*

THE END

Printed in the United Kingdom
by Lightning Source UK Ltd.
201